Beyond Divorce

Brenda Hunter

Beyond Divorce

A Personal Journey

Fleming H. Revell Company
Old Tappan, New Jersey

Scripture quotations not otherwise identified are from THE MODERN LANGUAGE BIBLE—THE NEW BERKELEY VERSION IN MODERN ENGLISH, Copyright 1945, 1959, © 1969 by Zondervan Publishing House, and are used by permission.

Scripture quotations identified KJV are from the King James Version of the Bible.

Excerpts from *Mere Christianity* by C. S. Lewis are Copyright 1943, 1945, 1952 by Macmillan Publishing Co., Inc. Used by permission of Macmillan Publishing Co., Inc.

Excerpt from "Spring" by Edna St. Vincent Millay is from COLLECTED POEMS, Harper & Row. Copyright 1921, 1948 by Edna St. Vincent Millay and used by permission of Norma Millay (Ellis).

Excerpts from *God in the Dock* by C. S. Lewis (edited by Walter Hooper) are Copyright © 1970 by The Trustees of the Estate of C. S. Lewis. All rights reserved. Used by permission of W. B. Eerdmans Publishing.

Excerpt from *The Four Loves* by C. S. Lewis is used by permission of Harcourt Brace Jovanovich, Inc., the publishers.

Lines from Emily Dickinson are from *The Complete Poems of Emily Dickinson*. Ed. by Thomas H. Johnson. Published by Little, Brown and Company.

Library of Congress Cataloging in Publication Data

Hunter, Brenda.
    Beyond divorce.

    1. Hunter, Brenda. 2. Divorcees—Biography.
I. Title.
HQ814.H84   301.42'84'0924 [B]   78-745
ISBN-0-8007-0903-9

Copyright © 1978 by Brenda Hunter
Published by Fleming H. Revell Company
All rights reserved
Published in the United States of America

TO Don, my second husband,
lover,
friend.

A good man.

And to Lynn and Kathryn, who
have been with me through it all.

My beautiful children.

Contents

Acknowledgments

Without the affection and persistent encouragement of a few people, this book might never have been written. It is with gratitude that I thank:

Doretta, a friend and neighbor who, when typing the early chapters late at night, encouraged me to keep going so that she could gain some perception about her own divorce;

Kay and Don Riggan, who read the manuscript and, from the first, believed in the published reality;

Marty and Roy Clanksy, good friends and surrogate parents, who called long-distance often to find out how the book was going;

Don, who edited every page and daily encouraged me to believe in myself.

Preface

Ironically, this book, which is primarily about my separation and divorce, has been written from the shelter of a second marriage. Before I remarried, I tried for two years to write this personal odyssey, but the words refused to come. Now the book has almost written itself; in fact, I have felt driven to get the ideas down on paper before the old memories go. As I savor the love of my second husband, it becomes increasingly hard to remember the pain of divorce. Time is, as they say, a great healer. So, too, is the love of a good man.

Why have I told my story, recounting feelings and events that most would shroud with silence? I have done so because I remember how desperately I looked for any help, any comfort, during those early days alone. Since I had no confidante, I turned to books, as has been my lifetime custom, to look for answers. I found nothing that spoke to me. The books that talked of the divorced woman whose primary goal was to ensnare yet another man repelled me. I was lost somewhere between marriage and divorce and, thus, I longed for someone to address my pain, my condition. Nothing existed in the late 1960s; at least nothing that I was able to uncover.

I have written this intensely personal book because I find myself telling my story to men and women, individually and in groups, who are alone. Most that I meet are in pain. They are involved in a struggle to create meaningful lives for themselves and their children, to deal with bitterness, to make ends meet, and to comfort mourning children.

In writing this book, I have intended to provide some broad perspectives on divorce and to offer hope. Hope is hard to come by during the early days and months of aloneness. But hope exists. It comes from knowing that divorce has a beginning and an end. The pain recedes in time, and a new life gradually unfolds. It is indeed possible to create a vital life as a man or woman alone, to raise stable children, and to love again. This time, if we have grown, the new love can be richer, deeper than the first.

This does not mean that each divorced person should remarry, or that remarriage, as Morton Hunt implies in *The World of the Formerly Married,* solves the problems generated by divorce. I do not believe this at all. Just as any first marriage should be entered into with great care, so should remarriage be considered with greater care. The stakes are higher because of the personal pain already experienced, and the difficulties posed are definitely greater. Some people believe that the presence of children from a former union and the shortage of money make remarriage hazardous at best. But all who are divorced must go on, must move out beyond divorce, with its anger, bitterness, and pain. This is imperative in order to establish a new life and identity as a single person.

A word about my former husband, Thomas. While I wished to write this book without references to him or our life together, it has been impossible. But I need to point out that this book is my story, my truth. Thomas has his own story and it is, I'm sure, quite unlike mine. Also, the first husband in this book no longer exists. While the man is very much alive, he is far different from the husband I knew and lived with for nearly seven years. He is years older and is now someone else's husband and the father of another child. Because we share two beautiful children, Thomas is still on the periphery of my life; however, he is a stranger. I know little about the man he is today.

I wish him well. With the hatred and bitterness largely behind me—for I was left—I feel able to be magnanimous. The wounds caused by the death of our marriage have, to a great extent, healed. And I am eager to move on.

Among the divorced, there are essentially two categories of people: those who leave marriages and those who are left.

Those who leave marriages may have their guilt, but those who are left definitely have their rejection.

Who recovers first?

Beyond
Divorce

1
September Friday

The heart asks pleasure first,
And then, excuse from pain;
And then, those little anodynes
That deaden suffering.

EMILY DICKINSON

I shall always remember that Friday morning in early September. At approximately 9:00 A.M. the phone rang, and an unknown male voice said, "Mrs. _____?"

"Yes?" I responded.

Without any introductory statement, the man said flatly, "Your husband has asked my wife to marry him."

"Who are you?" I demanded, lowering myself into a nearby chair.

He continued, "Your husband and my wife work together at the medical center. For the past several months they have had an affair, and yesterday my wife told me that she intended to get a divorce in order to marry your husband."

The man proceeded to tell me his name and remind me that we had met at a party in his home the preceding Christmas. As I listened to his calm recital, my mind rejected his shattering statements. Finally, I told him that I did not believe him and hung up the phone.

With mounting fear, I immediately dialed my husband's number at the medical center where he, a physician in training, worked. Thomas was a first-year resident in one of the most prestigious programs in the country for his particular specialty. When Thomas calmly answered his phone, I told him that I had received the most preposterous phone call from a Mr. B., who said that Thomas had asked Mrs. B. to marry him. "You certainly did not, did you?"

Thomas's voice remained calm. Without answering my

question, he told me to engage a sitter for our small children and that he would come home immediately. He refused to give me any reassurance over the phone, but said we would talk later.

I should have been forewarned by his refusal to answer my question and by his willingness to come home at nine-thirty in the morning, but the need to deny the validity of this hideous revelation kept the truth at bay.

The next thirty minutes were among the longest of my life. With shaking hands, I called the sitter and made arrangements for her to care for our two daughters. Lynn was seven months old at that time, and her sister Kathryn was two and a half years old. As I waited painfully for Thomas to drive the thirty miles home, I tried to think.

What does one think about when disaster hovers at the borders of one's life, threatening to destroy? As I stood watching for Thomas's car, my mind registered some truths but at the same time practiced denial. Surely Thomas had not had an affair. He came from a Christian family, was a graduate of a Christian college, was himself a nominal Christian. He was the kind of person who was safe. Besides, we had agreed early in our marriage that if we ever ran into deep marital trouble, we would not involve a third party, but would, with decency, deal with the marriage first.

And suppose he had had an affair. Surely he would have chosen one of the available single women at the medical center, not a married woman, who would first have to untangle her own marriage before she married him. When could he have found time to have an affair? He had been home each night that summer. Naively, I did not admit the obvious: One can always find the time to have an affair.

Even as I denied the possibility of the affair, another line of reasoning went on at a deeper level. I acknowledged that during our six-year marriage the last two years had been full of anger, resentment, and coldness. Any meaningful communication had broken down, and I did not know who Thomas was anymore. We no longer shared our deeper thoughts with each other. Thomas had retreated into some hidden place, and I had become an angry woman who often greeted her husband filled with resentment.

All that summer we had lived together in a particularly painful state because Thomas had begun to speak of a temporary separation. He was unhappy in our marriage and felt that our growing marital pain necessitated a separation. I asked him to reconsider and, as far as I knew, he had made no definite plans to leave the marriage. There had certainly been no mention of another woman.

When Thomas finally arrived, I was frantic. While he drove to a nearby meadow and parked the car, I questioned him with growing terror. Thomas remained silent until he had stopped the car. Then, turning to me, he said deliberately, "Brenda, it is true that I want a divorce. It is also true that I want to marry Linda." He then proceeded to tell me about his relationship with this coworker.

They worked on the same floor at the medical center. Linda was a nurse, and as she worked with Thomas he apparently found in her the supportive listener that he lacked at home. What had started out as conversation over coffee became, during the summer, a full-blown affair. Now both wanted to end their present, impoverished marriages and begin a new life together.

I could hardly believe his words. I begged him, I implored him to reconsider. "What about our children?" I asked. He simply countered that it would be better for them to be raised in peace with one parent than in tension with two. "But there need not always be tension," I countered. "We could get help; you did at one time love me, and I still love you. We could go to a marriage counselor or a psychiatrist."

Thomas stated that he had made an irrevocable decision to leave the marriage. I did not believe him for some time. Nothing, I felt, was irrevocable. But I was wrong. It appeared that he had decided months, even years, before to leave the marriage, and I was talking to a man who, for all intents and purposes, had gone away.

I was deeply and profoundly devastated. Monogamous to the core, a nominal Christian, I was committed to my husband and to our marriage. No feminist, much of my identity came from being Thomas's wife and the mother of our two children. Besides, divorce was anathema to me. While I knew that we were deeply unhappy (and I denied the full extent of it), I did not believe that the solution to our marital and personal problems lay with divorce. We were, Thomas and I, educated professionals who knew about the helping professions. Why not use them?

Moreover, I had invested six years of my life in this relationship. I had supported Thomas financially for some of his medical training, and we had struck an uneasy bargain: I was to put my emotions on ice, particularly during his internship, and when the years of training were over, things would get better. We were never specific about what the things were, or how much better they would get. But somehow I was supposed to be his supportive wife, even when I needed emotional support and found little readily available.

No one can put his emotions on ice. I hadn't been able to do it during the internship and had grown angry at a husband who was seldom there emotionally, even when he was there physically. Thomas hadn't put his emotions on ice, either—he had become fed up with an angry wife and had, it seemed, started looking for a supportive woman. His need had driven him to another woman, who had thoroughly displaced me in his life. Now things would never get better. We were going to be divorced.

I reeled through the hours. First I felt a numbness, and then a cold, icy terror. I knew I was totally unprepared to face the future alone, with two babies in tow. I ached for my children, because I had been raised by a single parent, a widow, and I could still feel and taste the loneliness and hardship of that kind of life.

Further, I had no job and had, in fact, left a full-time teaching position at a southern black college so that we could move north for Thomas's residency training. Even though I had searched for another full-time teaching job, I had found only a temporary and exploitive position at a junior college.

Moreover, I had, or so I thought, few inner resources. My time as a suburban housewife with babies had eroded my self-confidence. The preceding year had been especially bleak. It had been a time of virtual isolation on a street occupied by depressed women.

Finally, I could not bear to think of raising the girls alone. What would I do when they became sick, had discipline problems, cried and whined their way through childhood? I was overwhelmed by the negative possibilities that loomed large.

Fortunately, relatives came for the weekend—it was Labor Day—and they endured the holocaust with us. They provided some sanity and stability during those early hours, when it seemed that my life had ended. Their presence also tempered my husband's resolve to leave immediately. Before the weekend was over, he had decided to remain in the marriage awhile longer, ostensibly so that we could get psychiatric help and thereby discover what had gone wrong in our marriage.

But Thomas made no promises. He did not say how long he would stay, nor did he agree to end the relationship with the other woman. Although he did acknowledge that the heart of the problem lay with the two of us, never was he willing to forgo the promise that the second relationship offered. Rather he said that, for the present, he would not actively pursue the involvement. Whether he made these concessions out of guilt, because of family pressure, or because of internal conflict, I do not know. I only know he stayed, and it would have been better if he had gone.

What followed was a unique kind of torment. Since Thomas made absolutely no commitment to the marriage, we lived together in an uncertain state. My anxiety knew no bounds; I did not know if he would leave in a day, a month, a year. I could not grieve, rage, or plan. Because I felt the marriage had to be saved, because I was terrified at the prospect of life alone as a single parent, I became frantically approval seeking and in the process lost my self-respect.

During this time I learned a bleak lesson: If one party wants to end the marriage, it cannot continue. When one half of the marriage wants the marriage finished, it is a *fait accompli*. The other party can stall for time but cannot by effort of will force the marriage to continue. But the party who is determined to leave the marriage should go, and go quickly. The one who wants the marriage to last prostitutes his integrity by agreeing to do almost anything to perpetuate the union.

And what about the other woman? Word had it that she and her husband had separated and were pursuing a divorce. She was always there, a shadowy figure just offstage, waiting to walk on if I forgot my lines or let rage momentarily engulf me.

What my children did during those months I do not know. I had been nursing the baby, but with the onset of the crisis, my milk began to dry up. I remember one of the early days, when I vacantly stared out of the window while Lynn nursed. I looked down at her with surprise and knew that in my grief and pain I had forgotten that she lay in my arms.

It soon became apparent that Lynn was missing out on my love and concern. She gained no weight for several months after the revelation of the affair, and this troubled me. Sensing my anxiety, she grew quiet. I grieved because I was unable to give her the quality of mothering that I had given her sister. It was just that my world had fallen apart, and I did not know how to mend it.

Our life together became a cold and literal hell, punctuated by ugly battles. We had no moment of peace. When Thomas finally left after seven months, it was with sadness and relief that I watched him go. While I desperately wanted him to stay (I was afraid that separation would necessarily precipitate a divorce), I knew that I simply could not endure any more of that way of life. But what new life was I beginning? I did not know. Without chart or compass, I was lost in the deepest suffering of my life.

2
All My Piled-Up Ruins

Thus the Lord comforts Zion; He comforts all her
piled-up ruins . . . .

Isaiah 51:3

When my husband and I finally separated after those seven
anxious months, I was alone for the first time in my life. I have
mercifully forgotten the terror that accompanied the realiza-
tion of my aloneness in the universe. Marriage is a state that
allows us to deny our existential aloneness; it is indeed possible for both men and women to leave home or college for
marriage and never learn to be alone until death or divorce
severs the union.

It was an awe-filled moment when I realized that I was at
the helm of my life, steering into dark and unknown waters.
My situation was accentuated by the absence of close family or
friends. My family lived hundreds of miles away, and only my
husband's family knew the truth about our situation. I could
not bear to tell mine. Further, we had no close friends. Our
marital problems had driven us into secrecy and isolation, so
that when our nuclear family was hollowed out, I was truly
bereft.

For a time, however, all my energies were consumed with
grieving. I felt as if I had been physically dismembered; my
body looked intact when I looked at it (which was seldom), but
some vital part was missing. I noted an empty space in the
center of my chest cavity that was there, intermittently, for a
long time.

I discovered that, in grieving, my life was reduced to its
most elemental level. My goal was simple—to get through the

day. I remember reading a book about grief, which stated that in deep grieving, one should not attempt the enormous task of getting through the whole day; one should merely attempt to live through the hour. And so I made it through those early days of separation one hour at a time.

Pleasure, when it existed, was of the simplest kind. It was spring, and I sat on my back steps reading Job and savoring a cup of coffee. The warmth of the sun thawed my frozen grief just a bit, and the coffee warmed my injured body. I read the Book of Job at that time because I knew that at least one other person had been where I was and had survived.

We had separated just before Easter, but nature did not cheer me. Outside was newness of life; inside was death and dying. A marriage was being accorded a funeral, attended, it seemed, by only one witness. As the flowers bloomed and the earth swelled with warmth, I identified with Edna St. Vincent Millay's bitter poem, "Spring":

> To what purpose, April, do you return again?
> Beauty is not enough.
> You can no longer quiet me with the redness
> Of little leaves opening stickily.

Life had indeed become "nothing," an "empty cup," "a flight of uncarpeted stairs," as the poet proclaimed.

I discovered that, for me, loss experienced through separation, with its anticipation of divorce, was worse than loss generated by death. My father and grandfather had died, and the pain that surrounded their dying was less than the pain I now felt. Death at least allows for the idealization of the departed person. Who has not heard widows speak in unreal terms of their happiest of marriages? In the same way, I had idealized my dead father throughout most of the years of my life.

But in separation and divorce idealization is impossible. The estranged spouse lives on the other side of town or the universe, and if there are children, he is usually a continuing presence in one's life. Since Thomas went through the ritual of visitation twice weekly, I had no sooner gotten over Sunday than Wednesday was upon me. Each time he appeared at my door, the sick patterns of interaction continued.

In addition, I learned that the end of the marriage signified even further loss. Not only had I lost a husband, I had lost nearly nine years of my personal history—the years of courtship and marriage. While death allows for the retention of good memories, the separated cannot at first afford the luxury of remembering the good times. The pain is just too great. Remembering the ugliness of the end conjures up great anger and bitterness. That, too, is a luxury in the early months, when energies are consumed in grieving.

It is only when substantial healing has been accomplished and one has gone on down the road that one can afford to remember the marriage. And even then, who can brush away all the sadness and reclaim the marriage in its totality? Rejection forecloses that possibility.

Most of us have known, at some time, the bitter sting of rejection. Thomas's rejection of me had been thorough. Not only had he left me, but he left me for someone else. I had to absorb the injury caused by a husband's repudiation of my self and my values, and I had to deal with the comparisons that the other woman's presence engendered. My response? I hated Thomas with a ferocity that surprised me.

The emotion was so intense that for a time it seemed as if I were in a yawning pit, with no possibility of escape. Perhaps my reaction seems extreme to some. I can only write from the perspective of one who had married her first and best love, whose commitment to the union was as total as she could make it. Thomas had looked upon my gifts, my person, and found them wanting.

I know there are those who have friendly divorces and who deny ever having hated a former spouse. They speak of the growth that has ensued since their divorce, and this somehow justifies the divorce itself. As I have listened to them talk, that former spouse sounds more like a distant relative than a first husband or wife. Some who herald their friendly divorces, when pressed, admit that they did not love their former spouses and are not sure why they married them in the first place.

This is not to say that I believe my experience is the norm. I know my early life left me ill prepared to end a marriage lightly. I had experienced my father's early death as abandonment and had known some rejection from one of the significant adult figures in my life. It was therefore impossible for me to objectify Thomas's rejection and see it as his problem. I had been left and, consequently, I felt at first that I deserved his rejection.

But I could not fully accept that idea; and so, in addition to the pain, I felt rage, which was, in the main, repressed. Since I hoped for reconciliation even after a lengthy separation, I refused to let the anger out. Some leaked out when Thomas came around, but most of it was internalized and surfaced as depression. I only began to get over the depression when I confronted my rage in the presence of a psychiatrist.

Thus, for a period of some months I spent most nights face down upon the carpet or gazing out at the uncomprehending night sky, engaged in the deepest suffering of my life. At that time a man lived close by whose wife had committed suicide, leaving him with four small children to raise. Sometimes, when I drove by his house after dark, I saw him gazing out at the night. I felt some unspoken kinship with him; we were both members of the fellowship of the bereft.

Some people go the bed-and-bar route at this juncture, or leap into a second marriage. The ego wounding is so great. My morality would not allow the antidote of casual sex, and I knew that if I ever married again it would be much later, after substantial healing had occurred.

And so I endured. I was grateful that I had been a literature major in college and had read Greek and Shakespearean tragedies. Before me were the examples of Oedipus, Lear, and others. They reminded me that pain and suffering were part of the fabric of human existence and that flight was not a viable answer.

Besides, I made a promise to myself at this time: Even if I moved forward at turtle speed, I would experience my feelings honestly and would never again prostitute my integrity or self-respect. I would grieve and, in time, rage; I would confront my inner ugliness and beauty—all the cowardice and all the possibility. And I would create a meaningful life for myself and the children. When I moved forward, I would never have to cover the same ground again.

I knew that in time I would have to deal with two honest children and answer all their questions. Early on, I decided not to tell my children lies or half-truths or to lie to myself about the future consequences of my actions: I did have a future, and my actions did have consequences.

An event of deep significance occurred during this time. Two months prior to that eventful Friday in September, I had flown to my mother-in-law's home for a brief visit. Thomas had just mentioned his desire for a temporary separation, and I was in turmoil. I needed to get away and think.

Alone in my bedroom, I acknowledged that my marriage was in a sorry state and that I desperately needed help. To whom could I turn? I turned to the only possible source of help for such deep human problems: I turned to God. I had been a nominal Christian since adolescence but had lived out the days of my marriage without God's presence. At that time I offered what I was to Him and asked for His help with my ailing marriage.

I know now that I wanted the continuance of my marriage above all else, even more than I wanted a close relationship with God. I had no idea that this simple, uneventful transaction would be the death of Brenda, of all she held dear. Nor had I any idea of the good which God would usher into my life in the next five years. My back was against the wall, and I simply had nowhere else to turn.

God, I later found, honored that private transaction in my

mother-in-law's bedroom. He did not spare me the consequences of past actions, nor did He allow me to manipulate
Him with my prayers. He did not at any time violate Thomas's
freedom of will, no matter how earnestly I bombarded heaven
with prayers for reconciliation. Instead, He began to teach me
to live an increasingly responsible, honest life. In short, He
helped me grow up.

But why was God seemingly so far away during those seven
months of marital agony and the subsequent time of deep
grieving? To the reader of this chapter it might seem that I
survived that time because of dogged endurance or the fact
that I had been a literature major in college. In truth, God was
there, inhabiting the hours with me.

In retrospect, I can see that He was the Person who kept me
from flying apart during that time. Unseen, unfelt, His was the
presence that provided the courage to move out, the hope
when human hope was gone. There were, I feel, two reasons
why God was not more real to me: First, the pain seemingly
cut me off from God; second, I did not know what to expect
from this relationship.

Although I punctuated the hours with desperate prayers,
grief anesthetized me. For a time all feeble energies were
consumed in an effort to make sense out of my life and live
through the day. The continual interaction with Thomas
added to my inner desolation.

And God? God was *out there*. I believed that I was utterly
alone with my pain. I expected little from God. My prior
Christian experience had not led me to expect much divine
interaction with my human life. It was only when the pain
abated and the world began to press in on me again that I
sensed God's movement in my life. And as He moved, life and
I started to recover.

3
The Vulnerable First Year

For the Lord has called you when you were an
outcast woman and grieved in spirit, and as a
woman in youth who was rejected, says your God.
For a brief moment did I forsake you, but with great
compassion I will gather you.

Isaiah 54:6–8

For more than a year I experienced life alone in suburbia
and found little support or caring. I soon came to see that the
life-style of the separated mother alone in suburbia was inhuman. In truth, my children and I led emotionally impoverished lives. They required far more nurturing than I, as a
single parent, could possibly provide. I desperately tried to
care for the children's needs, but no one cared for mine, except God, and sometimes it seemed that He resided on some
distant planet.

Yet life remained to be lived or endured. Since I needed
money to support us, I soon located a job and a baby-sitter and
made the decision to remain in the same house until I had
some sense of direction. By this time the children had known
nearly a year of parentally induced chaos, and they needed
some stability. I knew, however, that I would have to move out
in the near future.

Since I had taught college-level English for two years, I had
no trouble locating a full-time teaching job at a high school in
the next town. That year was horrific. My baby greeted the
dawn until she was two years old. Since she wanted to do little
more than chortle at that early hour, I did not get up with her
immediately and instead wore out a hair dryer trying to drown
out her noise. It was with guilt that I plugged in the dryer and

left Lynn for her roommate, Kathryn, to cope with, but I did it anyway.

C. S. Lewis writes about the waking moment, when all the pain rushes in, in *The Grief Observed*. Some mornings all I could mutter was, "O God, how am I going to make it?" One friend said a year later, "Brenda, I did not believe you would survive."

But survive I did. For nine months I was a full-time working mother. I was up at 5:45 A.M. to dress and feed three people. Then I dropped the girls off at the sitter's before driving thirty miles to work. I picked the girls up at 3:00 P.M., cleaned the house, fixed supper, bathed and put two tired little bodies to bed. When Fridays came, the day that regularly ushered in a lonely weekend, we three had supper at Howard Johnson's so that I could sit in a room full of people. Only at the latest possible moment, when the girls were bone weary, did I turn the car homeward.

I marvel at the schedules of some divorced women. They must have tremendous energy and drive in order to live their lives. After a year of working full time, I made a decision that has shaped my career plans. I decided that I would never again work full time, if I could avoid it. I would rather have a short working day and live on a limited income than submit myself and my children to an inhuman schedule. Sadly, some women do not have this option.

Because of my schedule and my continuing inner pain, I had little to give to my children. Fortunately for the girls, I found a wonderful woman to function as a surrogate mother. Margaret was herself divorced and had raised three children alone. She was cheerful, loving, and energetic—a contrast to my depressed self. She enjoyed both girls, and the baby soon grew to love her. In fact, the day came when Lynn cried because she had to leave Margaret's arms for mine. That stung. Yet even with this good care, Kathryn grew quieter and sadder, and it increased my unrest to see pain mirrored in the lives and faces of my daughters.

It makes me angry to read authorities who blithely suggest that a one-parent home is far superior to a home fraught with difficult marital problems. This had been one of Thomas's presuppositions. The implicit assumption is that the single-parent home is peaceful, and that living alone, the custodial parent can put his or her life into order quickly, and adequately meet the needs of the children.

However, it usually takes divorced people some time to straighten out their lives. Since personality healing seldom occurs on schedule, who will care for the children while Mother comes out of depression, tries out various life-styles, or puts her life into a new order? The father? Unless the order is reversed and he is the custodial parent, the father is off doing the same, only with greater freedom of movement. It is an irresponsible society that encourages unhappy parents to seek divorce as the only viable solution for personal problems, with little regard for the children of these unions.

What some women or men may need during the early months when they reorder their lives is a surrogate parent who will step in and care for the needs of the children until the mother or father begins to again function adequately. I was deeply grateful for dear Margaret, the surrogate mother God provided for my children, but at the same time was deeply conscious that I was missing out on my children's lives, particularly Lynn's.

To counter this, sometimes at night when Lynn lay awake long after Kathryn had gone to sleep, I would go in, pick her up, and bring her into the living room to rock her. As I cradled her in my arms, I sang softly, "All Through the Night." When she smiled up at me, I felt deep sorrow: How I longed to get in touch with my children's lives once again.

Later someone shared the Old Testament verse which says of God: ". . . gently He leads those that are with young" (*see* Isaiah 40:11). I longed for some kind of care and protection for me, so that I could adequately mother my children. Yet all of my energies were consumed with work, the maintenance of a house, the physical care of small children, and the arduous task of restructuring a life.

During the time alone, I learned that while I had no man to care for me and the children, God intended to care for us. He became my "husband," as the Bible says in Isaiah 54, the chapter I have retitled "God's Care for the Woman Alone." While I was uncomfortable with the image of God as husband, I came to see that He could provide all that a good husband would render: care, love, and the proper environment for personal growth and fulfillment.

This was clearly in evidence one particular night, when Lynn became ill and began to moan with pain. The hour was late when her cries gained intensity. This was one of the few times that I tried to call my husband at his apartment; I thought that he, a doctor, could advise me, for I was afraid that she had some acute abdominal problem. In truth, I was still psychologically dependent upon him and wanted his comfort and help. He was not at home.

In desperation, I dialed the pediatrician's office, little expecting a response. By this time it was midnight. Unbelievably, he answered and told me to bring the baby in, so that he could check her. The three of us drove to his office, only to discover that Lynn had an ear infection. She was medicated and soon began to quiet down.

As I rose to leave, I expressed my gratitude and surprise that he had been in his office at that late hour. "You are really lucky," he said. "This is the only night this year that I've worked this late. I came in tonight to do my income tax." As I drove home, I knew that what had just occurred was no coincidence. We were without husband and father, but we were not alone in the universe. God cared for us. As I climbed into bed for a brief sleep before the next day's work, I was profoundly comforted.

That first year alone contained another hard experience: For the first time in my life, I came close to having an affair. Since I was hurting and lonely, I was vulnerable to any male attention that came my way. Although I did not go looking for comfort, I found it readily available in our society. It is a truism that if one is unhappy, one can find a listening ear and, ultimately, a willing partner somewhere. Usually the willing partner is himself unhappy.

This man was married, and he had recently learned that his wife had had an affair of some duration with his good friend. Because he loved his wife, he had been deeply hurt by this experience. For a brief time he and I toyed with the idea of a sexual involvement, because we were physically attracted to each other. Fortunately, at this time I saw two people weekly: a psychiatrist and a Catholic nun. Although an unlikely pair, these were the two people God had placed in my life as a survival unit to help me through that first year.

I eventually told both about the temptation the relationship posed. The psychiatrist counseled sanity and asked that I examine my motives. Was I attempting to get back at my husband for his affair? Admittedly, that was a significant part of the motivation. Also, it was logically part of my friend's motivation as well. I found it hard to admit that I was not the sole reason for this man's attentions.

It was good that I talked about this relationship with these people. If I had been secretive, I would probably have gotten deeply involved and later regretted it. As it was, the whole experience was injected with a bit of humor.

Almost every Saturday night I drove to the nearby convent to have coffee and talk with my friend, Sister Dorothy. I was a Protestant, but met this gracious woman when I attended a weekend conference at the convent some time before. She had been my counselor, and the relationship soon deepened into friendship.

At the time I was contemplating getting physically involved with Jim (I was already emotionally involved), I had the flu. After a day of steady vomiting, I prayed that God would get me to the convent, which was thirty miles away, and keep the interior of the car clean. He did.

Once inside the old mansion, I told Sister Dorothy what I was considering, while I spent my time either lying on a sofa or running to a nearby bathroom. She listened, laughed, and gave me a soda. She said with simplicity and without condemnation that she knew I would not continue the relationship with this man because of the depth of my faith in God.

She was right. By Monday the flu was gone and the moment of contemplated passion had passed—for both of us. My friend and I agreed that we could not violate our morality simply to hurt our spouses. He had to deal with his life and I had to sort out mine and make some decisions about the future.

I realized then that the first year alone is an extremely vulnerable time and that the separated person needs all the help he can get to keep from injuring his self-respect.

While the culture states that human needs can best be met in a series of sexual relationships, I discovered that was not so. There are other ways to meet human needs, without going the route of casual sex. What we need when we are recovering from a broken marriage is not more problems: We need love, acceptance, and someone to interject hope. We need someone to say that we can have a full life, raise stable, happy children, and love again in time. Affirmation is best found in relationships with stable, loving people in a friendship or, ideally, in a Christian community. It is not found in the experience of casual sex, where two needy people come together, each seeking affirmation. It is woefully hard for two half-filled cups to fill each other up and have anything left. It is indeed impossible.

During that first year I paid a psychiatrist to be my friend, and he openly acknowledged that this was one of his functions. I do not deny the invaluable help that I received in Dr. Johnson's office, where I cried, raged, talked, and in the process regained a sense of my personal worth. He helped me to more clearly understand my husband's personal problems, and at the same time he helped me begin to deal with my own. He encouraged me to be properly responsible for my actions and to refuse to accept undeserved blame from Thomas.

Primarily, however, he talked to me. Since I was coming out of a marriage to a rather silent man, I refused to pay a therapist to sit quietly, hour after hour. While Dr. Johnson admitted that he usually said little to his patients, he agreed to respond to me. Some of the things he said were quite significant and strongly influenced my thinking. He helped me to see that out of my past came great strength, as well as much pain. If I had not been a strong personality, I would not have survived some of the difficulties of my early life.

Doctor Johnson also coffronted me in the areas of my personal irresponsibility. He stated that I could not expect my husband to come home frequently to an unhappy, angry woman and do nothing about it. He noted that I did not take responsibility for my feelings, but tended to blame my unhappiness on medicine or my husband or our limited income.

I, who am somewhat cynical about the whole psychiatric profession, learned two important things through this encounter. First, the value system of the psychiatrist is communicated to the patient, no matter how loud the therapist's disclaimers. Even if the therapist says little, it is important for the Christian that the doctor is, if not a Christian, at least sympathetic with the values Christianity propounds. Mine was.

Second, treatment takes about as long as the therapist and the patient agree that it will take. One should be wary of unspoken contracts and should ask the therapist how long he envisions that treatment will continue. The question about the length of treatment has been one of the well-kept secrets of the psychiatric profession.

After about a year, I was ready to move on. I had invested about $1500 of my own money in treatment, and I did not want to spend any more money on therapy. Also, my inner life was growing increasingly lonely and sterile. I felt as if I were a lonely Christian, struggling in what modern theologian Francis Schaeffer calls "A post-Christian world." Permeating each gesture was the thought: There must be more to life than this.

4
In Search of Community

My Lord God, I have no idea where I am going. I
do not see the road ahead of me. I cannot know for
certain where it will end.

THOMAS MERTON

I had been a coward all my life. When I lived with Thomas,
the prospect of driving thirty miles in freeway traffic, accompanied by crying babies, unnerved me. Yet after fifteen
months alone, I gave up a secure teaching job, sold a home,
car, and furniture, and moved to London, England.

It all came about because of a book that I read during the
early months alone. While I was grieving, I was also casting
about for a more human life-style.

A friend sent me a copy of *L'Abri* by Edith Schaeffer, and
immediately after I finished the book, I wrote to the Schaeffers
and asked them if I could come to Swiss L'Abri with my two
children. One of their daughters answered my letter, stating
that the Swiss government was granting fewer long-term visas
and that L'Abri was not set up for visiting children. Priscilla
did suggest, however, that I attend the first L'Abri conference
in Lookout Mountain, Tennessee, in March. Perhaps there I
could talk to her parents and get some further ideas about
Christian community.

Why had I written to the Schaeffers? I was moved by the
integrity of their faith and their willingness to move out, trusting God to provide a work for them and the necessary funds to
support that vocation—all without the gimmicks so often associated with faith works.

Edith and Francis Schaeffer, motivated by God, had acted in

39

a highly original way—they had opened their home on a Swiss mountain to whomever God might bring to their door. Doctor Schaeffer, a former midwestern minister, and his wife wanted to provide a spiritual shelter (the French word *l'abri* means "shelter") for the people who came to their home in Huèmoz.

At first only a few people came, but later, when the news of L'Abri spread by word of mouth, the people came in greater abundance. Today literally thousands of people from around the world have been to one of the L'Abri's that exist in England and four European countries.

Here was a couple who not only believed that Christianity was true, and therefore relevant to twentieth-century individuals, but who had moved out into the unknown without a program, without financial backing, and without advertising. They simply prayed for their needs, and God answered. Here was a quality of belief that I had seldom witnessed, either during my years at a prestigious Christian college or at any of the churches I had attended thereafter.

And so, when March came, I left the children with their father and flew to Lookout Mountain to attend the L'Abri conference. I knew no one at the conference. Nor did I know exactly why I was going, except that I had to find some viable alternative to the life-style I was experiencing as a woman alone in suburbia.

At this point God engineered an interesting chain of events. My seating partner on the plane was from London, and when I mentioned my interest in immigrating to Europe, he spoke eloquently about life in England. Although I was not considering England at this time, I listened politely.

The L'Abri Conference was held at Covenant College, and about five hundred people attended. As God would have it, I always found myself in the cafeteria line behind those who knew the Schaeffers and L'Abri well. One woman had taken her children to Switzerland, and she encouraged me to do the same. Another had been divorced, and to her I admitted that I felt like a maverick among so many apparently happily married people. She understood.

And at the end of the conference, I cornered Francis Schaeffer and asked for thirty minutes of his time. Sequestered in the library with this gracious man, I told him my story and said that I was looking for some form of Christian community. He told me about the Ealing, London, church/house and stated that people were buying and renting houses and flats close to the church at 52 Cleveland Road. Francis Schaeffer suggested that I might find the Christian community I was seeking in Ealing. In addition, we talked about divorce, telling the children the truth about my situation, and remarriage.

I learned later that people had written months in advance to request thirty minutes of this man's time. I was gratified that God had given me this brief time with Dr. Schaeffer, because it proved invaluable as I began to make plans for the future.

As I flew home, I was not yet convinced that we three should move to London. Nonetheless, I wrote to the minister at the Ealing church and asked about life in England and the possibility of moving there. His return letter was cordial but discouraging. He stated that rents were high and that one could not get a work permit unless a job had been secured before entering the country. Strangely, I was not deterred by his response and put my house on the market shortly after the conference.

Need drives one relentlessly and requires a response. I *needed* to find a more human life for the three of us. The first year alone had awakened a longing for a life with connections, and I simply could not continue another year rooted in my sterile, suburban life.

About this time, I had a moment of heightened perception as I drove down the freeway. I knew that if I opted for security at that time in my life, something vital in me would die. I believed I would experience a diminishing spiritual life, for my faith could not endure in isolation any longer. Besides, I

was incredibly lonely. Although I had managed to live by my
ethical code thus far, I knew that if I stayed where I was, I
would soon accept the cultural answer for loneliness: a man in
my bed.

But still I hesitated. And as I wavered, God gently encouraged me to trust Him. A significant event occurred during the
spring that once again involved the girls' pediatrician. As he
was examining the children, I told him that I was considering
a move to London. Since he had gone to school in England, he
was delighted and added that I should meet a friend of his, an
English physician who taught at a local medical school. No
sooner had he spoken these words than the phone rang, and as
he talked, I realized that the person phoning was this same
physician. Coincidence? Hardly. Before I left the pediatrician's office, I had the promise of a dinner invitation with the
English doctor and his American wife.

The dinner proved to be important for two reasons. First, I
learned a lot about life in London through an American woman's eyes. Later this information proved immensely helpful
during the early, hard months in England. Secondly, I was
given hope for a better life in the future. I noticed that the
couple, who appeared to be in their forties, had three young
children. When I rose to leave, the woman, obviously happy,
followed me to my car and stated some things that I had not
known: That she, too, had been married to a professional in
training, had been divorced, and had nearly fallen apart during her first year alone in New York City. She met and married
her present husband when they were both thirty-three;
further, the children were products of the second union.

I sang all the way home. Here had come encouragement
unbidden; here was a fellow traveler who had gone on to a
richer life. I believed that God sent those two people to encourage me to move to England and to believe in the good
future He had planned for us.

The decision to launch out into the unknown was finally

made one morning while I stood in the high-school library, reading *Thoughts in Solitude* by Thomas Merton. Although I had been gathering my forces so that I could move out, Merton's words triggered an immediate response. In speaking about laziness and cowardice as two of the greatest enemies of the spiritual life, Merton stated: "And sooner or later, if we follow Christ we have to risk everything in order to gain everything. We have to gamble on the invisible and risk all that we can see and taste and feel."

Within the hour I had resigned from my job and had begun to make concrete plans to move the three of us to London. My principal discouraged me, saying that the teaching market was already flooded and that I would not be able to find another teaching position upon return. He was right. I was not able, years later, to find another job as a teacher; instead, I found another career that I liked better. So it is when we risk the little that we have, which is our everything, to follow God.

Having made the decision to leave the country, I began to dispose of the artifacts of my marriage. The house was quickly sold and the furniture was carted out of the door, piece by piece. My husband came to remove the last vestiges of his life there: medical books, tools, some camping gear. It was with anger and sadness that I watched him pack up his car.

He said little and showed no visible sadness. I wanted, even at that point, to engage him: to speak about some topic of mutual concern, to know that he, too, was suffering, to ask him to come back. But instead I spoke only words of anger. Feeling frustration and a deep despair, I realized that it is hard to end a marriage. The cords of love and hate that bind us together are strong and defy easy severing. So Thomas drove away, and I turned back to the practical problems involved in a transatlantic move, feeling empty.

I had made reservations to fly to London on the first of July, in order to avoid the backyard Fourth of July celebrations, but by Monday of the week that I was scheduled to fly out, the closing on the house had not occurred, nor had I sold my car.

Praying frantically and feeling a bit punchy, I walked into the local supermarket to buy groceries and saw the manager, a cheerful, older man who sometimes joked with me. I asked him if he wanted to buy a car. "Sure," he said. "What kind?" I pointed to a yellow Maverick that sported a huge dent in its trunk (I had backed into a tree), and within two days the manager was the car's new owner.

When the closing on the house was postponed until Wednesday, just twenty-four hours before I was due to fly out, I panicked. How could I get everything done and make the plane, particularly when all of my money was coming from the sale of the house? What if there was a further delay? By this time, I did not have the psychological wherewithal to change my plans at the last minute. My babies were exhausted, and so was I. I still had to dispose of a washing machine and dryer and pack our few belongings.

I had no recourse but to trust God. At this point I learned a valuable lesson: When I make plans and think that what I am doing is His will, I submit the plans to Him and am willing that He change them, even at the last minute. At such a time, I exert whatever faith I can muster and watch as God takes me down to the wire. He always does. Things fall into place, but often at the last possible minute.

So close to the wire did He take me that when the moving van came to move the new owner into the house, I had not yet moved out. I returned home from the bank to discover that two men sat on my lawn. My mother-in-law, a wonderful, strong-minded woman, had told them, with a laugh, that they could not move furniture in because we were not ready to leave. While the disgruntled men waited outside, this woman, whom God had sent to help me pack up a marriage, was inside, chuckling, hard at work.

When my mother-in-law's car finally pulled out of the driveway, it was stuffed. We could barely see out of the back window. All that I had left from my marriage was inside her car: some silver, pots, paintings, books, and two frightened, beautiful children. I felt both sadness and exhilaration at leaving that house—I was sad that an era of my life was thus ending, exhilarated that a new beginning lay ahead.

5

Expatriate With Two Small Children

> . . . I found him nearest when I missed him
> most; I found him in my heart, a life in frost, a light I
> knew not till my soul was dark.
>
> GEORGE MACDONALD

It was 2:00 A.M. when I finally helped my weary children onto the plane at Kennedy Airport. There had been a severe summer rainstorm that evening, and we had waited for an hour in heavy traffic only to discover, when we finally arrived at Kennedy, that our plane would be four hours late in leaving the airport.

That piece of news depressed me, for it had been an exhausting day. The early portion of the day had been spent packing my mother-in-law's car and moving out of the house. A friend drove us to the airport, but when she discovered that our plane would be delayed, she excused herself to go home to her waiting husband and warm bed. How I envied her.

The moment after Helen left was incredibly lonely and frightening. I looked at those two babies I had uprooted from a familiar setting and watched them try to sleep on the hard plastic chairs in that sterile airport, and wondered what on earth I was doing to them and to myself. Lynn, whose diaper bulged under her plastic pants, was a mere two-year-old when her mother became a self-styled expatriate. Kathryn, another little blond, was a responsible four-year-old, who was used to helping me carry Lynn's paraphernalia. She seemed to accept the fact that Lynn was often carried, was most often on Mommy's lap. While Kathryn accepted this as a part of her young life, I longed for her to have a father who would carry her occasionally. She was too young to forgo this protective parental gesture.

The hours inched by. At last we were able to board the plane. No sooner had I changed Lynn's diaper and awkwardly bedded us down than the stewardesses began lifting the window shades to admit the morning light. I did not sleep during my first transatlantic flight, for I was overcome by a quiet, gnawing terror.

Although friends had commented on my courage in moving out into the unknown, particularly in the face of a negative response from Ealing L'Abri, I knew in my soul that the whole venture might turn out to be absolute folly. Surely I felt that God was leading us, but I could not be positive that I had interpreted all of the signs accurately. Only time would tell.

My husband did not try to stop us from going to London. He had left New England as well, to pursue further training, and he had agreed, with some reluctance, to send the monthly support check to London. I had no idea whether or not I could live on this monthly allotment; it certainly would not support us in America. But this was 1970, and England had not yet joined the Common Market. Word had it that one could live more cheaply in England than in America, and I was counting on that.

It was with great effort that I guided two sleepy children off the plane at Heathrow Airport, while at the same time carting both a diaper bag and a bag of toys. We had to wait in yet another line for the immigration authorities to check our passport and stamp our visa. At last we boarded a double-decker red bus and headed for our downtown hotel, where we would finally go to bed, hopefully to sleep.

I soon discovered that moving to another culture, even an English-speaking one, is difficult. The time change and the trip left us weary for days. Since it was summer, the sun shone until late at night, and the girls had to adjust to going to bed in bright light. The weather was cold and the currency was hard to get used to. At first I spent pounds like dollar bills and grew poorer quickly.

I was uncomfortable with the density of the population in London and nearly grew claustrophobic in the tube stations when bodies stampeded on and off trains. The vocabulary was different, and we had to learn to speak English rather than American: *bonnet* for "hood" of the car, *chemist* for "pharmacist," *petrol* for "gas," and on and on.

Since I wasn't sure what direction to take, I telephoned L'Abri, only to discover that Dick, the minister who had been my contact, was away. So there we were in London, knowing no one and not sure what to do with ourselves. I did not know whether I would stay for three weeks or three years. With much inner desolation, I realized that I had cut all ties with my past and had no home to return to. Our possessions consisted of three pieces of luggage and three boxes of toys.

Having nothing better to do, I decided to tour England. I had read literature in college and graduate school, and the prospect of seeing the places I read about excited me. I rented a Volkswagen and pulled out onto the street that runs parallel to Hyde Park, sitting on the wrong side of the car, driving on the wrong side of the road. For about a week I bounced off curbs because of my difficulty in gauging distances from the new position in the car.

The girls and I drove hundreds of miles throughout England and Wales. It was fun to see Shakespeare performed at Stratford, to drive through the Lake Country and stand in Wordsworth's tiny house, to see Oxford and Cambridge.

But after several weeks, the ordeal of getting in and out of a different bed each night nearly shattered all of us. Lynn seemed bewildered by the constant change of scene, and while I was gratified to see Stonehenge at last, she wandered among the monoliths unhappily until she spied some familiar cows in the background. Then she crowed. Kathryn said that she missed her daddy, our green house, her kittens—all left behind in some other world.

Once, as we rode near Glastonbury, I started to tell the girls an abbreviated version of the Arthurian legend. Kathryn burst into sobs when I came to the end of the tale and Arthur's death. "Don't ever tell me any more about King Arthur," she said. "He reminds me of my daddy." It became apparent that she thought that her daddy, like Arthur, was dead, and only after many conversations did she seem to understand that her father was simply in another place in America. For several years after that, she refused to listen to the story of Arthur. It conjured up memories, buried, but still painful.

When we arrived back at L'Abri in Ealing, I was ready to admit defeat and fly back to America. The church in Ealing acted as if it did not quite know what to do with me. I was not some frumpy, middle-aged woman, and for some unknown reason this, I was later told, was what they had expected. And Christian community? To the newcomer, *community* appeared to be a goal, rather than a reality. Granted, many people were beginning to buy houses and rent flats near the church/house, but a shared life? Few seemed to have any conception of what that would entail.

Sensing my growing despair, some came to my aid. One of the elders said, "Brenda, don't doubt in the dark what God has shown you in the light." He added, "And if you feel you must return to America, call us first." I appreciated his words. I learned later that we had been prayed for at the evening prayer meeting.

The next day a woman came to my hotel door. When I responded to the knock, a tall, attractive woman said, "Hello. I'm Katie, and I've come to take you to my house for breakfast." She leaned down to talk to the two little girls peering up at her. "Do you like cornflakes?" Lynn and Kathryn nodded, and we were soon on our way to Katie's home. Little did I know that dear Katie was giving me the first of many rides in her gray car. She would in time become one of the closest friends I have ever known.

While Katie kept the girls, I went house hunting with Lillian, a woman who had raised her daughter alone. Lillian and I discovered a flat which rented for fifteen pounds a week, around thirty-eight dollars at that time. The flat was decorated with old, shabby furniture, but it was shelter and a stable home.

We moved in the next day and confronted the task of creating a new life. At first I had real difficulty getting used to a rather primitive life-style. If I wanted to cook or have any heat or hot water, I had to feed coins into a gas meter. Heaven help me if I ran out of ten pences. I had no vacuum and had to cart our laundry several blocks to the laundromat. I had to shop three or four times a week, since we had a tiny refrigerator. Eventually, I came to enjoy the whole process. After grieving, it was therapeutic to have so much time taken up by the rituals of living.

When the daily rituals became more familiar, however, I began to cast about for something meaningful to do with my hours. Granted, I planned to participate in the community life at the church/house, and I wanted to get close to my children. But I was an educated American woman, who felt driven to accomplish something of significance with her life.

At that time I felt that I either had to work, at least part time, or pursue a Ph.D. in order to be a worthwhile person. Since I loved teaching on the college level and was limited by having only the M.A., it seemed feasible and wise to go back to graduate school. Having rather grand aspirations, I applied to Oxford, Cambridge, and the University of London.

But God had other plans for my life. He started to show me, with great gentleness, that I had some erroneous ideas about the direction my life should take. In the first place, I needed to realize that I had not geared my academic life for high-powered professional training or graduate education at the more prestigious universities.

During college I was content just to make the dean's list each semester and did not drive myself to attain high grades. I enjoyed graduate school and did well academically but decided to have a baby rather than forge ahead, as my advisor urged, and complete my Ph.D. first. So Kathryn was born before I received my M.A., and I was nursing her at the time I sat for the Master's exam. In fact, I left the exam early to rush home and nurse my baby. While I passed the exam, I did not impress the committee with my brilliance.

Thus, I attempted to storm England's academic bastion with only a good second-class degree and vague ideas about a possible Ph.D. topic. I did not know when I applied that these particular universities select candidates who have both a first-class degree and a firm idea about a dissertation topic. I was rejected by Oxford and Cambridge. One of the colleges at the University of London tried to coax me along until I could come up with a viable dissertation topic. I never did.

Second, though I loved to read literature and thought I would enjoy working on C. S. Lewis, George Macdonald, and Tolkein as mythmakers, I knew in my heart I did not have the ability required to become a literary critic of these writers, two of whom had shaped my thinking and fed my soul. Nor did I have the inclination.

Finally, Thomas's rejection had hurt so deeply that I felt driven to prove that I was a worthwhile person, and the way I sought to do this was through further education. This was one more attempt to deny Brenda and embark on a course of action that would render me more acceptable to the people in my life. It was not until I arrived at L'Abri that I received something I desperately needed and had seldom found in the human arena: real acceptance for who I was. At L'Abri I had no credentials to commend me; no longer a doctor's wife, I was simply Brenda. For one of the few times in my adult life it was, thank God, enough to be Brenda.

As I began to be known and loved by various Christians at L'Abri, and as the graduate programs were no longer options, I was finally able to turn my full attention to the mothering of my children. While my children had always been loved, their needs had clearly been of less importance than my own driven need for professional growth and personal fulfillment. As work and graduate school faded into the background, however, I started to see my children in a new way.

I saw how deeply they experienced the loss of their father and their familiar home. I saw their sad and confused faces and was touched. As a result, I started to spend large blocks of time with them and to respond to their real needs in a far more tender, nurturing way. It is just not possible to compassionately care for our children when our heads are elsewhere, either involved in our own pain, or consumed with thoughts about our own fulfillment. As I gave those girls top priority in my life, after God, many of the good feelings I had sought via professional growth came as the reward for good mothering. Over time, the children—who had come to L'Abri with sad, frightened faces—relaxed and blossomed. As I witnessed this unfolding, I was deeply moved, and determined that they would never again lose their place of significance in my life.

6

A Time of Healing

It is not simply to be taken for granted that the
Christian has the privilege of living among other
Christians. Jesus Christ lived in the midst of his
enemies.

DIETRICH BONHOEFFER

We have a basic, although often unacknowledged, need for
community. Human needs cannot adequately be met in a relationship of two. Witness the breakdown of the nuclear family.
When two people try to meet each other's needs in total, they
end up feeding upon each other, and the relationship is hollowed out. Or if they pursue separate lives, each will become unbearably lonely. There is, divorced people attest, no
lonelier place than inside a bad marriage. Our needs for vital,
shared experiences require the larger family, or community.

When my marriage ended, I knew that the nuclear family
had failed me, or I had failed it. As a single parent with unmet
relational needs, I believed that my survival depended upon
finding a place where a larger community was a reality.

That place turned out to be Ealing, London. Today it seems
strange that God led the three of us an ocean away, to a group
of struggling Christians, to find our niche. But that is precisely
what happened. Those two years in Ealing were among the
best of my life. What made this time so valuable, so memora-
ble? Never have I received so much love from so many. What
that small group of Christians gave to me and to my children
can never be taken from us.

I went to London with no grand ideas about participating in
the formation of a community. I went, quite simply, with deep
need. I had, however, made a substantial commitment to that
unknown community simply by turning my back on my old

life. Without a home or job to return to, I banked on the success of whatever experience awaited us in London. In looking back, I'm sure that the degree of my commitment played a great part in the ultimate success of the venture.

I went to L'Abri soured by the organized church. Having attended a Christian college, with its ritual of daily chapel, I had been saturated by a certain brand of Christianity. Later, after I graduated from college, I hated to go to church. Church seemed so divorced from the rest of my life. The Sunday social outing alleviated my guilt (I felt I should go to church), but I did not know the church people well. Nor would I have dreamed of sharing my needs or concerns with them.

With the breakdown of my marriage, however, I returned to the church, hoping to find help or meaning there. What I found were Sunday coffee relationships and little else. Thus, L'Abri was my last effort to find anything real within the organized church. If the Christians there had been cold, disinterested, uninvolved, I would have returned to America disenchanted and absolutely bereft. As it was, I found not only a real church, but a therapeutic community as well.

I believe that the church, when functioning properly, can provide healing for those who come. Within the church exists the necessary structure, the philosophical framework, and the power to deal with people and their problems. The power exists in the Person of the Holy Spirit. But the church members must be willing to give up their isolation and total pursuit of material comfort in order to become involved in other people's lives. This is the only way out of loneliness and into community.

We were by no means a homogeneous group as we crowded into the cold living room of the church/house for Sunday services. Among us were the conservatives, the unemployed, the educated, and the uneducated. There were those straight people whose lives had taken an ordinary course; there were those who had been everywhere and done almost everything. But as we met together, what mattered most was the fact that

God had drawn us all together for His own reasons.

And what did we, who came with our diverse needs, find at 52 Cleveland Road? We found Christians who believed that in order to have community they must live physically close to one another and spend time together. Many lived within walking distance of the church. Some shared flats and houses. I was surprised to find single people sharing housing with couples. This was certainly not an American custom.

In addition to shared housing, many shared vacations, money, and cars. We knew about one another's marital pain, impoverished finances, inability to discipline children, gifts, and responsible life choices. We prayed for one another and helped one another in practical ways. In time we learned to love and value one another.

As it turned out, I found at 52 Cleveland Road far more than I could have envisioned. I found Christians who were willing, at some sacrifice, to follow the Holy Spirit into a life of deeper sharing. Here were people who were committed to Christianity as a body of truth, to community as a goal, and to one another as persons to be loved. The L'Abri Christians, like those in the Bruderhof (a similar community I had visited in the States), realized that Christ provided the only bond between them, and they were sufficiently aware of the problems in the human arena to know that only the Holy Spirit, and not good intentions, could sustain the community experience.

The church was small enough that it was not necessary to organize dinner groups so that members might see one another regularly. Dick (our minister) and Mardi, his wife, set the tone by having different people into their home each week for meals. Soon others were sharing meals, going to plays or concerts together, working on projects of mutual interest, and babysitting for one another's children. What set this group apart from any that I had witnessed in the organized church was their willingness to become involved in one another's lives.

This involvement in other people's lives was not always

easy or pleasant. Life in community had its hard, dark side. Occasionally the very people seeking help would disappear, stealing money or clothing from people in the church. Dick had clothing and personal items stolen on several occasions, once by a young stranger he had taken into his home. Although sad and angry, Dick did not cease ministering to the community or to strangers who appeared at his door daily. In addition, life in community often required that one do something for another when one did not feel like it. Always it meant refusing to run away from difficult relationships.

When we see the same people week after week, and sometimes several times a week, it is hard to ignore a strained relationship. Just across the room sits the very person who has hurt our feelings or whom we have hurt. And because the community life is so valuable, and we will not leave it, we must make amends. Besides, it is hard to hide hurt or anger when two or three others know about it and are urging us to put the relationship right. In this process we become real to one another.

God taught me some beautiful things through the various relationships within the church. I arrived at Ealing L'Abri battle-scarred and convinced that most, if not all, significant relationships would dissolve in the face of conflict. Within a short time, however, I realized that these people were well aware of the problems of human nature.

They knew that people were sinful and that it did not take long for *niceness* to go. So they talked about the injurious effects of gossip, about forgiveness, and about the need to go to each other and make things right. I had never watched Christians actually practice confronting each other in love. I had heard lots of sermons preached about love, but what power is released in the community life when people actually practice loving one another.

One friend in particular brought healing to my personality. Ros, a psychiatric social worker, became my friend and, in the process, was one of the few people in my life who did not run away in the face of my negativism. One evening she heard me out and, in so doing, helped me begin to rebuild the trust that had been shattered during my marriage.

That night Ros listened patiently as I voiced my discontent, my doubts that God had anything substantial for us in London, my loneliness. In addition, she heard all the self-pity. When I finished the tirade, she said, "Brenda, you are going to have to make up your mind about whether Christianity is true or not, and live accordingly. Once you make this decision, you will need to exercise your will when you get depressed. Feelings are important, but so is your head. If you determine that Christianity is really true, then you need to trust God."

Ros was perceptive enough to know that I did not need sympathy, but she also knew I needed someone in my corner who would allow me to get the garbage out without feeling rejected. That night Ros gave me a great gift. Thus, our friendship began, and it is not surprising that this has been one of the best relationships of my life.

In addition to Ros, I formed friendships with couples, which provided further healing. I feel that separated and divorced people need to relate to couples, and not just to the single population. One couple spent more time with us than any other. These two were Katie and Barney, who took the three of us into their home and into their lives. Katie was aware of my needs, my moods; she chauffeured us around when need required it; she helped discipline my children. And when her husband, Barney, was in town (he traveled a lot as a BBC cameraman), the two invited the three of us for unnumbered meals.

What was best about this friendship was the complete acceptance I received from Katie and Barney. I hid little from them. They listened as I voiced my bitterness about Thomas and Linda, my cynicism about men, my fears about the future. And they opened up with me. We were friends in the truest and best sense. I felt at home in their presence.

Those two had a rare gift. Since they were so committed to

each other, and over the years of marriage had grown comfortable in each other's presence, I found that I, too, felt comfortable and at peace. Few people have achieved this quality in their marriages or within themselves. How I grew to love these two friends. And as they gave me their undivided attention on numerous evenings, the wounds caused by rejection began to heal.

And what about the children—how did they fare in community? Lynn and Kathryn now had many adults interested in their lives. Susie gave them swimming lessons, and she and Will took them on picnics. Judy and Bob included the three of us in their family holiday in Devon. Lillian knitted several of those warm English sweaters. And Bill saw them as children who needed time with a male friend.

The children blossomed during our time in Ealing. I came to see how imperative it is for children to have the larger family to relate to. Particularly when they live with a single parent, the children need an extended family, so that they are not always thrown on the limitations of that parent. Other adults flesh out the custodial parent's view of the world. In a shared life children find what children in America found generations ago when relatives lived nearby to share in the child-rearing process. They have many teachers. Since we transient Americans no longer have the extended family, we must create our own larger family. The shared life of a Christian community can do this beautifully.

God gave us a family at L'Abri such as I had never known. In the extended family of my childhood there had been glimpses of the love, the compassion, the commitment I found in Ealing. But in Ealing, these qualities stood out in bold relief. Why? Simply because of Jesus. His love reached out to me in my loneliness through a variety of unique and beautiful people. Later when I saw the same joy, witnessed the same commitment in other Christian communities, I realized anew that the people did not create the atmosphere. Fine as they were, it was the Holy Spirit who filled the community with love, joy, and compassion.

And it was the Holy Spirit who encouraged me to go inside myself and, using George MacDonald's image, "scrub the floor of my cell." For the first time, I started to ask questions that required hard, honest answers. And as I confronted my role in the death of our marriage, I was able to see the union itself with greater clarity.

7

Confronting the Self

Can it be any comfort to them to be told that God
loves them so that He will burn them clean? . . .
They do not want to be clean, and they cannot bear
to be tortured.

GEORGE MACDONALD

Which of us wants to be exposed and afterward burned
clean? We like our familiar darkness, our elaborate self-
justifications, our defensive posturing. And yet when we submit our lives to God's scrutiny, He begins to show us what we
are. Little by little, His inexorable love illuminates the hidden
corners of our lives, and He begins burning away our evil
deeds. The process, which is ultimately redemptive, is ini-
tially painful.

When God began to expose my secret thoughts and motivations, I did what countless separated and divorced people do.
I turned away from the examination of my own actions and I
focused completely on my husband's deeds. During that time,
I became a compulsive talker. Obviously, I talked to carefully
chosen people: relatives, friends, a therapist, and eventually a
minister.

The minister, Dick, was one of the first to brush aside my
verbiage about Thomas and concentrate on my responsibility
for the death of my marriage. During our conversations, Dick
pointed out, by references to various Psalms, that our emotions
honestly reflect the state of our inner and outer life. It would
have been wrong for me to feel happy when my life was up-
ended. While my depression was obviously a reaction to the
loss of my husband, an identity, a way of life, it was also di-

rectly related to sin in my own life.

What was the sin that produced the depression? Beneath the surface lay enormous anger and resentment against various significant figures in my life. While the connection between anger and depression is a rather traditional psychiatric interpretation, it was not until I arrived at L'Abri that I saw the relationship between my legitimate anger (with its bedfellows, resentment and self-pity) and deep inner sin.

For years I had felt my anger was justified. It was related to feelings of self-pity and the overall attitude that, because of my difficult early life, God owed me a lot. My father had died when I was very young. My mother and I wrestled with poverty and her anger at God thereafter. More recently, my only marriage had ended with rejection and abandonment.

Thus, I was an angry woman. How often I symbolically shook my fist at God over the years, and how I nursed those wounds and grievances. Most of the time I kept them so far out of sight that I believed them gone. Since it was untenable for me to express this rage to the people who incited it, I kept it inside until it finally surfaced as depression.

Over the years I have learned some things about anger. Although the Bible gives no detailed prescription for handling this volatile emotion, it does acknowledge its presence on both human and divine levels. Christ felt anger, and on occasion the anger of God burned against His people in the Old Testament.

The Bible does encourage the keeping of short lists and tells the angry person not to let the sun go down on his wrath. Our anger should be short-lived and dealt with. Psalms 37:8 says bluntly: "Quit being angry, and dismiss fury; do not get heated; it leads only to evil." We know from reading Ephesians 4 that while this chapter acknowledges that we will get angry, we are urged in verse 26 to "commit no sin," and later in the same chapter we are admonished to get rid of anger and its fruits. In addition, we are told to be kind and loving to one another.

This is, however, a difficult task. The best antidote for current anger is to lovingly and firmly tell the person who provokes the anger that hurt feelings exist. If this is not possible, then one has an even harder task. Some say that they give their anger to God, and He takes it away. Some attempt to push their anger into the background, only to find it surfaces later as bitterness and resentment. Since resentment is harder to eradicate, I find that it is best to go to the person, as we are told in Matthew 18, and attempt to restore good feelings to the relationship.

At L'Abri we attempted to tell the truth in love. We were encouraged to confront each other, with the understanding that both parties were committed to listening and to forgiving each other. There were several beautiful occasions when I went to various people, confessed my anger and resentment, and asked for their forgiveness. On each occasion, I was granted forgiveness immediately, and the relationship was healed.

While God is well aware that we feel anger on occasion in daily life and need to deal with it rather than repress it, He also wants to heal our old angers. He wishes to lance old wounds and cleanse us from hatred. In my life He has done this through a two-pronged process: first, through forgiveness, restitution, and more-responsible living patterns; second, through the healing of memories.

God straightened up my outer life before He healed the old, but not forgotten, wounds. Through various conversations with Dick, I examined self-pity, a great producer of anger. Said Dick, "Self-pity is psychological suicide." He went on to state that ingratitude lies at the base of self-pity. God, he pointed out, owes us absolutely nothing, no matter how difficult our lives. He loves us, and He has always been present and aware of all the pain. But nonetheless, our proper response to life is gratitude for all His gifts. As Dick and I talked, I became more aware of the connection between good feelings and responsible living.

Like many in our culture, I had given feelings too much significance in my life. While I had listened to my feelings for years, I had all but ignored the fact that feelings are transient and are directly related to behavior. It was not until Thomas said that he no longer loved me that I saw clearly the connection between feelings and behavior. We had not treated each other lovingly for a long time. How could he have felt deep love for me? Feelings of love are fragile, and they respond as directly to callousness as they do to tenderness.

Moreover, I learned that while we need to own our feelings honestly, as we slog on and act more responsibly in a given situation, eventually we will feel better about life. This was illustrated once when a neighbor came to talk about the difficulty she was having with her eldest daughter, who was surly and pushed her divorced mother as far as she could. The neighbor realized that she needed to handle her child's misbehavior directly, rather than push the unpleasant child away. When she acted in a more responsible way with this child, the child responded rapidly and became more loving. Later this woman said that, as a result of disciplining her child, her feelings toward the child had improved markedly.

Possibly the most responsible act that I engaged in after my arrival at Ealing L'Abri was that of dealing with broken relationships in my past through the power of forgiveness. Not only did I need to forgive those who in some way had injured me, but I needed to ask several to forgive me for my bitterness toward them. Once again Dick was influential, and he encouraged me to examine my life, cease blaming others, and ask God to remove my bitterness.

This need to clean the slate, to grant and seek forgiveness, came to a climax during my last year in London. Although I had been struggling to forgive Thomas since my arrival at L'Abri, it was not until I met Sarah that this was accomplished. Sarah, a woman in her sixties, was reputed to be a wise woman. I spent only one hour in her presence, but those sixty minutes changed the course of my life.

From the moment I sat down in Sarah's tiny study, I knew that I was there by divine appointment. Sarah looked at me kindly when I gave her a brief history of my life, and with wisdom said, "Your problems with your mother antedate your problems with your husband." Then without further elaboration, she said, "Let me tell you part of the story of my life.

"I was the textbook case of the deprived child. When I was seven, my parents, who were missionaries in China, sent me to a boarding school at the other end of the country. From the age of seven until I was thirty-two, I spent about two years total time with my parents. Never did I see them in our own home—rather, we vacationed at the coast or at a nearby mission house.

"Just before I was forty, I was suicidally depressed and in rebellion against God. Since I was a Christian, God became my psychiatrist, showing me how deep my hatred was and how I had wronged others by my attitudes, particularly my parents. I saw in a new way that if there had been no one else who had sinned, my hate would have nailed Christ to the cross. I asked God's forgiveness, and then I knew I would have to make things right with my parents. The next time I saw them, I stated simply that God had shown me how wrong my attitudes were toward them. He had forgiven me; I asked them to forgive me. Although my mother responded beautifully, and our communication later became more honest and free, my father could not respond.

"Later, my father lay dying. I was miles from home but learned from my brother, a physician, that Father was agitated. As I wrote my usual weekly letter, I prayed that the Holy Spirit would give me a special message for him. I wrote the letter on Monday night, which was Tuesday A.M. in China. I told my father that I had forgiven him and now knew that he had forgiven me. I said that when we met in heaven, we could talk about it.

"He never received my letter. He died on the day it arrived. Yet from Tuesday morning he became peaceful, and remained so until his death. He said to my mother, 'Everything's all right,' but she did not know what he meant until my letter arrived on Saturday morning."

Profoundly moved by Sarah's story, I determined to rectify things in my own life. When I returned home that night, I was relieved that Gretchen, the woman who lived with us, was out for the evening. I needed to be alone. Retreating to my cold bedroom, I had a session with God. I dumped a lifetime of anger and self-pity before Him. I chronicled all the real and imagined abuses, wept because of the pain, voiced all the despair and hopelessness. Then when the garbage was out, I asked Him to forgive me. With the tirade over, I wrote to my mother and other significant people and asked for their forgiveness. These particular letters were well received; in fact, they marked the beginning of a more honest, more loving relationship with several people.

Forgiveness is the door to psychic freedom. We use valuable energy maintaining our bitterness. When we finally do go through the process of owning the wrongs, forgiving the people who hurt us, and ultimately seeking forgiveness for our bitterness toward them, we move out and find ourselves in a new place of sunlight and joy.

I have learned, however, that once is not enough. We must continually grant and seek forgiveness, as long as we live. Like certain shellfish, as we move through our days, we become encrusted again with anger and bitterness toward others. Periodically, we need to examine our souls and allow the Holy Spirit to reveal to us those people who need our forgiveness.

And what if one cannot seemingly forgive another person, no matter how hard he tries? I have had the experience of praying for years to forgive a particular person, only to feel that I had not succeeded. Then after a time, I suddenly realized that forgiveness had finally come. I could think of this person, of the event, and all the pain had disappeared. Thus, I believe that it is imperative that we are willing to forgive, even if it ultimately takes some time for the feeling of having for-given another person to come.

After I had learned some things about forgiveness, God was ready to show me yet another way to heal the past. I was surprised, years after forgiveness had been granted and re-ceived, to discover that, while I thought all animosity was gone, some old angers remained. After a deeper experience with the Holy Spirit, when He became a Person to me, I had several occasions when memories, long forgotten, surfaced.

Alone in my home, while sitting in a chair in my living room after a time of prayer, I relived several memories that were particularly painful. One had to do with the death of my father. Just before he was drowned, my father had taken me to his parents' home for a short visit, so that he and my mother could move into a new home. I was later told that I spent much time running to the window to see if he was returning to take me home. He never came back. Although I was two and a half at this time, I was deeply affected by the death of my young father. Later, as an adult, I became aware that whenever I waited for a loved person to return home, should I look out the window to see his approaching car, I was overcome with a deep sense of sadness.

On the day when I relived the leave-taking with my young father, I saw at last the correlation between this childhood event and my adult response of looking out the window for a loved person's return.

As I wept and relived that sense of lostness, I asked God: "Were You there when that happened? Did You, too, feel the longing, the sadness, the sense that the world would never again be the same?" Somehow I knew that God, as Father and hovering presence, had been present all the days of my life. Moreover, I felt then that He would redeem each event, no matter how painful or injurious, and use it for good. I did not know how this would be accomplished. *How* is not as impor-tant as *if*.

On subsequent occasions, always in the privacy of my home, the Holy Spirit has brought other long-buried, painful memories to the fore. Each time I have experienced a sense of God's guiding presence, and I realize that He has loved me from the cradle. I have become confident that God is vitally concerned with my inner healing. He can substantially heal us, and from the moment we begin to cooperate with Him, the moment we are willing to forgive all known wrongs, He, like a good physician of the soul, begins to lance our wounds.

Thus, I have found the years of separation and divorce a time of inner healing. As I have taken hold of my life, made restitution for wrongs, the whole color of my life has changed. Gone is the gray, and now warmer hues work to dispel any darkness.

The burning clean that I dreaded at the outset has been far different from my expectations. Perhaps I expected God's merciless light; i.e., His judgment, and what I have experienced is His healing love. I have learned not to fear the burning, but rather to turn toward the One who executes the whole process. The result of the burning? A different woman.

8
Why Did Our Marriage Fail?

> I asked him, "Have you put the marriage and the
> divorce into perspective?"
> He answered, "I shall probably spend the rest of
> my life putting my first marriage and subsequent
> divorce into perspective."
> A DIVORCÉ'S COMMENTS

From the earliest hours alone, I asked myself, others, the
four walls: "Why did our marriage, a union begun in such high
hope, end?" The answers have been a long time in coming.
Even now I am not certain that I know why our marriage
foundered and eventually died.

It is extremely difficult to examine one's marital failure with
any sort of objectivity. During the early months, I, like many
separated and divorced people I have known, spent much
time engaged in self-justification. At first, I believed that
Thomas was primarily responsible for the death of our marriage. Later at L'Abri, I started a process that led me to assume
more than my share of the responsibility for the failure of our
marriage. It was only after months of heaping ashes on my
head that I was finally able to look at the marriage as a whole
in an attempt to discover the weaknesses in the union itself.

I realize now that, from the outset, our marriage was a leaking ship. Externally, this was not apparent. Thomas and I were
like many college graduates in the early 1960s: We were
bright, ambitious, and full of hope. I graduated from the prestigious Christian college we attended with honors; Thomas,
with high honors. He had been accepted at a medical school in
his hometown, and I had secured a teaching position at a local
high school. We were married in June, one week after gradua-

tion, full of joy and expectancy. After all, we loved each other. For a time we believed that was enough, especially since we did not have the financial problems which many young couples face.

Internally, however, we were poorly prepared for the task of creating a viable marriage. For one thing, we came to the marriage with widely disparate ideas about conflict and problem solving. Thomas hated conflict. He felt the way to resolve conflict was never to have any. He had grown up in a home where feelings were seldom discussed and where all was apparently harmonious.

I, on the other hand, had grown up in a home charged with emotion, often too much so. I was comfortable with a certain level of anger, although I did fear uncontrolled rage. Since I was insecure in my ideas about anger and conflict, I tried to adopt Thomas's view and keep conflict at a minimum in our lives. Unfortunately, this was not always possible. We were, after all, two sinful people, and each of us wanted his own way a good deal of the time.

Moreover, we had few skills for problem solving. We were not able to discuss our disparate points of view, communicate any feelings associated with a particular issue, and come to some mutually agreeable solution. When we did fight, either Thomas withdrew early on and I joined him in an uneasy withdrawal, nursing my grievance, or I pushed the argument hard, until fatigue or the late hour made us call a halt to our feud. But nothing was ever resolved.

I do not recall that we ever arrived at a happy, mutually acceptable solution for any area of conflict. Granted, one of us may have capitulated early on, but resentment usually followed. Each of us felt he had been had. Never did we say we were sorry, nor did we ask or grant forgiveness. Instead, we collected what my lawyer called nonnegotiable brown stamps, and at the end of our marriage, our books were full.

What did we fight about during our marriage? During the early years, we fought primarily about Thomas's family, and the place they would have in our lives. I realize now that, from the outset, a major problem in our marriage was the fact that we did not establish sufficient emotional independence from Thomas's family.

I spoke to a counselor recently about this aspect of marriage, and he replied bluntly, "It has been my experience that unless a man establishes emotional independence from his family, in particular his mother, the marriage is in any real sense doomed." He added that a wife's dependence on her parents did not seemingly cripple a marriage as much as a husband's. Thus, the Bible enjoins the man, and not the woman, to leave and to cleave. Obviously, in a healthy relationship both partners need to focus on the new union, rather than the original family unit, as they create the foundation for a strong marriage.

In addition to our inability to establish emotional independence from Thomas's family, both of us felt we had unmet emotional needs stemming from our early lives. Part of our bargain with each other was that we try to be all that the other had missed out on earlier. As life would have it, we just could not carry it off. He could not be the father I had never known, nor could I always give blanket approval to all of his ideas or plans.

I have come to see that it is dangerous to promise the miraculous to any human being. I can be Brenda to another person. Nothing more. I cannot be mother, father, sister, brother, healer. Nor can any one person become that for me. God alone is my nurturing mother and guiding, affirming father. Only He can carry our neurotic dependency and heal those wounds from early childhood, once we relinquish our self-pity and come to Him for healing. But Thomas and I did not know this, and so we felt angry and thwarted in this marriage that promised so much and seemingly gave so little.

In addition, our marriage was founded on some romantic illusion that the feelings of love were all that life required to sustain a marriage. When the hard times came, love, as a feeling, began to be challenged. Within a year or two (it is hard to be precise about the decline of good feelings) those warm, intimate conversations that were there during courtship had ceased.

No longer did he wrap his arms around me in our bed and listen as I shared a wish or a painful memory. No longer did I want to give him all that he obviously needed. And those romantic longings that we both possessed? They went underground. As I coped with marriage to the real Thomas, I used to ride silently beside him on long car trips and have fantasies about emotional closeness with him. At such times I would lamely try to break the silence.

"Let's talk," I would suggest.

"What do you want to talk about? Give me a topic." His angry reply frustrated me, and so the silence went unbroken.

I had not bargained for the sterility and loneliness that inhabited the inner circle of our marriage. While communication had not apparently been a problem during the courtship, it became a critical problem during the marriage. I see now that what we communicated early on were the longings, the good feelings of love. We had no language to express our negative emotions. Since we had only one fight during the two-year courtship, we had not established a pattern for dealing with conflict.

When Thomas and I finally went to a marriage counselor for a few visits, long after our separation, it appeared that he never loved me or felt good about our union. The counselor pointed out that what had happened was that negative feelings had dammed up all positive responses to me. Thomas would need to express his negative feelings in order to rediscover any positive feelings of love. This never happened, because our trips to the marriage counselor soon stopped.

If we had turned to God at the point of our inner loneliness and disillusionment, our whole history might have been different. Thomas and I had reached a point in our marriage when feelings were simply not enough to carry the day, particularly when good emotions no longer abounded. We did not realize that any marriage, no matter how rich and deep, falls short of filling all the emptiness. The reason is obvious. God created us for Himself, and He preserves an inner space that remains forever empty until we finally, in despair about ourselves or our marriages, turn to Him. That inner space is a room that only He can inhabit. Once He is given His place, He begins to deal with the poverty of the marriage.

Since we had not given God the sacred place in our lives, Thomas and I idolized Eros. What happens when a couple idolizes erotic or romantic feeling? C. S. Lewis describes such a couple in *The Four Loves:*

> They expected that mere feeling would do for them, and permanently, all that was necessary. When this expectation is disappointed they throw the blame on Eros, or more usually, on their partners.

Since Thomas and I did not blame Eros for our marital unhappiness, we conveniently blamed each other. We were blamers *par excellence.* We started the marriage blaming others for the heavy stress between us. Later I blamed the goddess Medicine and eventually Thomas for the marital poverty. And he blamed me. I thought that if we only had more time together we could recapture some of the warmth of courtship and early marriage. He indicated that if he only had more freedom of mind to devote to his career, all would be well.

Our mutual blaming arose from our vastly different expectations for our marriage. Having been raised female, I, like many women in our culture, had been trained for an intimate relationship and wanted nothing more than a close union with Thomas. After our marriage, I longed for the closeness of courtship to continue and hoped that, even as a doctor, he would want to spend time with me. Having been raised male, he seemed to expect that once married, he was at last free to get on with the business at hand. Ambitious, he had been trained for academic accomplishment, and so he funneled his energies into medical school and did exceedingly well.

Family life in America does not train men and women well for the art of marriage. The male grows up used to Mother, who essentially cares for his needs and demands nothing in response. Why should she, when Father meets her emotional needs? The man marries and takes it for granted that the non-demanding physical and emotional care will continue, with slippers and newspaper waiting before the fire each night. His wife, who has a history of intimate conversations with her mother, a succession of friends, and her father, if she is fortunate, wants to experience the same closeness with her chosen husband. Thus, she grows resentful when he puts his needs for success continually ahead of her need for closeness.

What eventually happens? The man either grows angry because of his wife's demands and walls her off, or he grows weary and trades her in for a newer model. Some listen, grow, and later become more sensitive, but this usually happens after they have achieved that long-desired career success.

The wife, sensing her husband's insensitivity, has essentially three choices. She may push hard, escalate her demands, and thereby run the risk of being divorced. If she is a Christian, she may give her desires to God and let Him change her husband. Or she may take the traditional path for American wives and temporarily shelve her desires for intimacy. During her twenties and thirties, she can confide in her female friends and hope that someday Johnny will learn to read her heart.

The latter course of action is not without peril. It assumes that when the man attains career success, surfaces, and is ready at long last for intimacy with a woman, he will turn to his loyal wife. What sometimes happens is that he chooses a co-worker to share his middle-age success and his budding thoughts. Magazines frequently carry stories of famous men who shelve their wives of many years for the more scintillating and often younger coworker.

I was not cut out of the sacrificial pattern, so my divorce came after seven years, rather than after twenty. But I do not believe the sacrificial wife has any better answer than the demanding wife. Both may ultimately lose. The answer lies in establishing the right set of priorities for the marriage as a whole. To become the sacrificial wife is to capitulate to the husband's first priority—career. To become the demanding female is to insist on the fulfillment of the wife's first priority—relational closeness.

Ultimately, the chief priority in any human life is a relationship with God. That must come before the Protestant work ethic, sex, intimacy, children, whatever. Only when God has this place of preeminence can all else fall into place. And then—contrary to what the culture says—the union of a man and his wife is more important than family or success. Only as the right priorities are established can two people begin to enjoy a fulfilling marriage on a daily basis. The battle for the marriage is a daily affair.

Why did our marriage fail? A more realistic question might be: Why did it last for nearly seven years? Without God, without good communication, without establishing a close, independent unit, it is indeed surprising that we nearly reached the seven-year mark. What I have not mentioned are the good aspects of our union.

We started our marriage with high hope. We desired a long and rich life together. In addition, we shared broad humanitarian goals. Naively, we stated that we "wanted to help people." We were vague about how we would do this, but we spoke of becoming missionaries, or of adopting one of Thomas's patients. We even, ironically, talked at length about someday writing a book about marriage.

And we had our warm moments, which were interspersed throughout the years. When my grandfather died and I was seven months pregnant with Kathryn, Thomas missed some of his classes to drive me eight hundred miles to the funeral. As we pressed to arrive in time, we were close, united. And after the birth of each child, for a period of months intimacy returned, and the flame of hope burned a bit brighter.

What I can never deny is the fact that I loved my husband. I loved him throughout the marriage and for the years of separation and early divorce. Also, I believe that for a time he loved me. I do not believe he knew me well before our marriage, or that he saw me as I really was. The real Brenda was too direct, too assertive in some areas.

Thus, our marriage was full of contradictions. We loved each other, but we did not know how to live together in an atmosphere of acceptance, openness, and trust. Thomas made a comment on the day we separated that illustrates this dilemma. After I had driven him to a downtown hotel and accompanied him to his room, I started to weep about the utter wreckage of our lives. As if to comfort me, he stated, "Brenda, if I met you today I would still be drawn to you."

He was attracted to me, but he was leaving me. He loved me, but he would not live with me. Thus ended my first and—at that point—only marriage.

I have known many couples since we separated, a few intimately. Some have had psychological problems as serious as ours. Some have been immature and have come of age inside their marriages. Others have needed therapy, prayer, and God's healing to rebuild their unions. Each couple has gone on to a better marriage, while our leaking ship eventually sank.

What made the difference? God and a strong commitment to the continuance of the marriage. I have seen God preserve, defend, heal, and nourish unions between people not that different from Thomas and me. And I have heard the men and women admit that divorce just wasn't a viable option. They had to improve their marriages, because they refused to seek greener pastures elsewhere.

And as I watched these unions survive poverty, infidelity, insensitivity, I have come to believe that Thomas and I could have made it, if we had asked God for His help. It would not have been easy. We would have had to grow up, shoulder the responsibility for our own lives and feelings, learn to handle conflict and anger, learn to love each other more deeply. And in the process, we would have spared ourselves and our children incalculable pain.

9
Telling the Children Their Truth

When a man is, with his whole nature, loving and willing the truth, he is then a live truth. But this he has not originated in himself. He has seen it and striven for it, but not originated it. The one originating, living visible truth embracing all truths in all relations, is Jesus Christ.

GEORGE MACDONALD

We live in an age when many people no longer believe in the existence of absolute truth. Truth, morality—both are relative. If we strive to tell the truth, then we are accused of limited vision, unsound motivation. As divorced people, in particular, we are warned that we cannot possibly perceive the truth in our situation; our perception is too colored by bitterness and pain. And so we are told to tell our children little about the separation and divorce, or to whitewash our own or the absent parent's actions, so that the children will love us as parents and have few identity problems.

During the early aloneness, I encountered these ideas in the books I read and the conversations I had with various persons. I was so confused about what to tell the girls that at first I told them almost nothing. Rather than mouth words I did not believe, I said little. I did know, however, that I was committed to telling them the truth, but for a while I did not believe that truth, as I perceived it, should be shared with them. The truth was so painful to me that I doubted its healing properties.

Later at L'Abri, I was not only encouraged to tell the children the truth about our situation, I was also encouraged to believe in the existence of truth and absolutes, as established by the Bible. The L'Abri Christians stated firmly that the Bible was *true* truth, and that it set forth a consistent view of man and human behavior.

After reaffirming the existence of absolutes, I obtained a firmer hold on truth. First, I saw that the Bible clearly states that we are able to tell the truth. Proverbs 12:19 states, "Truthful lips endure forever, but a lying tongue only for the wink of an eye." Later in the same chapter, "Lying lips are an abomination to the Lord, but those who deal faithfully are His delight" (Proverbs 12:22). And the New Testament beautifully says that Christ is Truth, and He comes to lead us into greater truth, since truth is what eventually frees us.

Having established the existence of absolutes and the fact that God wants us to tell the truth, I was ready to speak to my children truthfully about the death of the marriage. But I pondered: What exactly do I tell them? Do I tell them that their father loves someone else? Do I share my pain with them? Do I speak half-truths out of some need to protect them or their father?

Since I had experienced the pain of the lie and the cowardly half-truth in my own life, I decided that although the truth might render greater pain for the moment, it would eventually heal. I knew that my children needed to have their perceptions of life validated: They saw my hurt and anger; they felt abandoned and lost. Their world was torn apart. For me to gloss over any of the ugliness and lie was to give them an untrue view of reality.

Obviously, my motivations were, at some level, tainted, and there was darkness in me. But I was all my little children had, and I was thus elected to speak the truth as best I could. I came to see that if my children were ever to trust me, if they were ever to be healed in their personalities, I must try to tell the truth—always.

The motivation was clearly there. When I saw the depth of their sadness and need, after I had straightened out my priorities and could thus turn my full attention to them, I determined that whatever happened, I would be a person they could trust. Trust in his parents is all that a young child has as he proceeds through life. And trust is a precious, perishable commodity. Once destroyed, can it ever be rebuilt?

I decided not to load them down with unnecessary details, nor to tell them all *my* truth. They were, after all, children, who had an inalienable right to be children and to love their other biological parent. But I determined never to tell them anything I would have to retract later. I would give a three- and five-year-old's dose of truth and flesh it out as they grew older. I suspected, and rightly so, that I would never stop answering questions about the death of our marriage. And so I told them *their* truth, as opposed to my bitter truth, hoping that as my pain receded, my answers would become more objective. In short, I did not seek to protect them from our reality, but only from my hatred and bitterness.

What was their truth? I felt they should know several things. Both their father and I were responsible for the death of our marriage. Equally responsible, we differed in our views of what to do with our broken marriage. Their father, and not I, believed that the solution to our problems lay in separation and possibly divorce.

Why had the marriage failed, they asked. I said that we had not included God in our union, and when troubles came like storms, our marriage crumbled. Their father, I added, no longer loved me and had found someone else that he now loved. Both wanted to know: Do you still love our father? I told them yes, but added that I felt much hurt and anger toward their father. And much mending would be needed if the marriage would ever function again.

I rejected the popular formula for telling the children about separation and divorce. The formula goes something like this:

> Your father and I have separated (and plan to get a divorce) because we argue and are unhappy. Your father no longer loves me, but he still loves you. Nor do I love him. He is not leaving (or divorcing) you; in fact, you have nothing to do with the separation. We both

love you, but we have agreed that the best solution for
our unhappiness, and the best thing for you, is for us to
end our marriage.

While there were certain portions of the formula that I could
endorse, I could not endorse several of the main tenets. Certainly the children were not the cause of our unhappiness or
eventual separation. I did, however, still love Thomas, and we
had not mutually agreed to separate. He simply left.

I did not want my children to grow up and assume that
because their parents had divorced each other, divorce was a
viable solution for their marital woes. Often divorce begets
divorce. I have known divorced people whose parents and
grandparents were also divorced. Thus, I attempted to give
the girls a Judeo-Christian view of marriage: I stated that marriage was a union created by God, in which both people were
to love each other until death. Moreover, marriage was often a
difficult state, and we all needed God's help. Only He could
teach us how to love each other well.

I told the children that divorce was not part of God's best
plan for any of us. God, however, allowed divorce because
sometimes we grown-ups could not, or would not, have soft,
forgiving hearts. I added that I certainly hoped that when they
grew up, they would not seek a divorce if trouble came to their
marriages (should they marry), but would try to solve their
problems in a loving way. We all agreed that separation hurt;
they missed their daddy and they hated to see their mommy
sad. Divorce, if and when it came, would also hurt.

We spoke about the pain associated with the loss of Daddy,
and many times we three cried as I held them on my lap. They
asked some poignant questions during those months when we
started to talk. Kathryn said, "When I marry and have babies,
will my husband leave me, too?" I assured her that she and I
were different people and that her father had not left me because I had had two babies; he left because he did not love me
any longer. What, they wanted to know, had I done to hurt
their father? I tried honestly to tell them. I spoke of my anger

and resentment, my lack of love. I could sense that they felt marriage was an impermanent state and that human love could not be trusted.

Thus, I tried to counter this anxiety by emphasizing what God could do with our lives and our marriages. While their father and I had shut God out, many of the marriages around us at L'Abri were warm and strong. Kathryn asked of one family, "Would Dick leave Mardi and Christopher?" I said that while anything was possible, I felt not. I believed, instead, that these people had a strong commitment to God and to each other.

I felt no obligation to paint a dishonest picture of their father, either to portray him as a loving man, reluctant to go, or as an unfeeling person who had abandoned his children. Books on divorce note that children get a large dose of their identity from each parent and cannot love one and hate the other without hating a part of themselves. Whatever my problems with Thomas, I was and am deeply committed to my children and want them to love and embrace themselves.

Also, I knew that as a Christian, no matter how deeply I had been hurt, I was as responsible for the death of our marriage as was my husband. And even though he said little, I knew that I had hurt him deeply many times in the marriage. In time I would have to ask his forgiveness, and I would have to forgive him.

Thus, I chose to be sparing in my comments about Thomas. It would be years before I could honestly support his actions as an absentee father, but even in the early, bitter time, I could support his biological position. And I have come to see how incredibly tenacious that biological tie is. Although they did not see Thomas for two years, when Lynn and Kathryn finally saw their father, they flew into his arms. On the basis of biology alone, Thomas has an impregnable position in the children's lives.

Although in the early years I tried to say little about Thomas as a person, I did give the girls a framework whereby they could form their own opinion of him. A frequent question that the girls asked was: Does our father love us? In answer to their queries, I read them portions from the *Boys and Girls Book About Divorce,* by Richard Gardner. Doctor Gardner suggests that a child can gauge the love that parents have for their children by finding out how often the parent wants to be with his child, if he is proud of his child, holds him, touches him, goes out of his way to be helpful.

Moreover, I felt that it was Thomas's responsibility both to tell the girls and to show them that he loved them. It was, and is, his responsibility as a busy physician to take the time to get to know the children when they visit him. From the early days I knew that I wanted to leave the arena altogether and allow the three of them to forge a relationship. Obviously, I would always have skewed vision as far as their father was concerned. Thus, I hoped that as I openly answered their questions, this would encourage the girls to someday talk to their father with the same degree of openness and, eventually, hear his story about the death of our marriage.

As a result of our conversations, the girls started to note the evidences of love from their father. They talked about the fact that he remembered their birthdays, all holidays, and he always provided financial support. I have encouraged them to be grateful for his financial provision and have been careful to point out that lessons, most of their clothing, and vacations come from their father.

Do the children believe that Thomas loves them? Sometimes. Most of the time they are not sure. But then there are the hours and perhaps the days when, unknown to me, they do not feel that I love them. I have learned just how vulnerable they are to perceived parental rejection. Once when Thomas called on Lynn's birthday and neglected to speak to her sister, Kathryn was crushed. "Why didn't he talk to me? He's my father, too." I was surprised at the immediacy and the depth of her pain. Although her father had never done this before, Kathryn felt immediately unloved.

The absent parent has a hard road to travel in convincing his children that he loves them. When he remarries, the children of the first union are even less sure of their place in the father's life. After all, he sees the children of the second union daily, and even little children can gauge what impact daily life has on feelings. And the absent parent who is idealized, feared, and who is, in some sense, a stranger, is seen as a larger-than-life character. His failings have deeper meaning than those of the custodial parent, who the child knows is frail, but will still be there tomorrow.

I feel, however, that the prognosis is good for a close relationship with their father. Obviously, any absent parent has to be consistent and work harder than the custodial parent to show his children that he loves them, but children are open and so in need of parental love that they will take almost any sign of favor, no matter how small, and wring it dry. Thus, I hope for my children's sake that a warm relationship is forged with their father. They need him, and I believe that he needs them.

And so, during that first year in London, we talked. I created a framework for subsequent conversations and have not had to retract anything that I have said. As the girls have grown older, they have asked new questions and have elaborated on the old. They have a more mature view of me, as a parent capable of frailty who is deeply committed to them, and they have an eagerness to know their father. They have a Judeo-Christian view of marriage, and are daily learning communication skills as we live a life of honesty with one another. As I see their open faces and clear eyes, watch them meet new people and situations with openness and trust, I believe that the rewards of truth telling are great.

The greatest reward is that they trust me. This was not always so. When their father left us, they were afraid that I, too, would leave, and for a long time their sense of trust in their world was shattered. For no matter how we try to soften it, children do feel abandoned by the parent who leaves, and

88

Beyond Divorce

they fear that the custodial parent will also leave.

One little girl, Janice, wrote a short paper at school that expressed her feelings about the absence of her separated father. Janice drew a picture of two tombstones which bore the names of her mother and father. While her father's tombstone was indistinct and off to one side, her mother's was flanked by flowers and the three children. Janice, who is eight, wrote: "I need my family because it is the only one I've got. And if my mother gose away we'v got nothing left."

My own children expressed their fear thus: "Daddy left us. Will you leave us, too?" It was some time before they truly believed that, barring death, I would be there tomorrow.

Since I realized how tenuous their trust was, I tried never to be late, to make no promises I could not keep, to do what I had said I would do. It was years before they stopped asking, "Will you pick us up at the time you told us?"

I always reminded them of our history. "Have I always picked you up at the agreed-upon time?"

"Yes," they said.

"Then you can expect that I will continue to do as I have done in the past."

We do not realize how vulnerable our children are in the area of trust and, consequently, how paramount it is for us to nurture trust by speaking the truth. I have known mothers who have sown seeds of lifelong mistrust by unthinking acts of cowardice. Each time we lie about the pain the dentist or doctor will cause, we can expect howls of betrayal.

Since I had not lied to my children in the area of daily life, perhaps it was easier to tell them their truth about the death of the marriage. I have always believed that children need to know what to expect from the events of their lives. Hence, whenever my children have had a painful event in the offing, I have prepared them carefully.

Obviously, I could never have told my children the truth about my part in the death of the marriage, could never have encouraged their honest and often painful questions, if God had not been showing me how to live an increasingly responsible, honest life. Although I had thought of myself as a basically honest person all of my life, it was only after I gave myself to Him that the dark corners of my soul were revealed. It was hard to acknowledge the self-deception and to confront the quiet, inner lies.

God alone is light; we are so much darkness. But He will draw us to the light and ask us: Can you bear to see yourself as you really are? I did it an inch at a time and have, even now, only a limited idea of all those areas cut off from view and awareness. Fortunately, it is God's business to expose our darkness and to call us to greater and greater accountability, coupled always with forgiveness.

But as we move out in the direction of truth and His warm, palpable light, we take our children with us, and over time we learn to tell the truth with greater depth and clarity. As we do, we—and eventually our children—are healed.

10

The Legal Divorce

Current American divorce law, as anyone who has
in any way been involved with it knows, provides
the widest possible range for the meanest possible
feelings.

JOSEPH EPSTEIN
Divorced in America

For the duration of one whole summer I waited to hear
when our divorce proceedings would occur. Since I had been
in England over one year, I no longer had state residence, and
so the divorce was to occur in the state where my husband
lived. I was fearful that whole summer, because I did not
know whether my having gone to England would prejudice
the judge against me in terms of custody or support.

God, however, gave me a special gift prior to those three
months of torturous waiting. I had always wanted to tour the
Continent, but found, even after moving to England, that I
could not afford such a trip. But God doesn't always wait until
we can afford to purchase our hearts' desires; He often gives
them to us when we are ready to receive them, or when our
need is greatest.

That April my Aunt Stella came to England and took the
three of us to the Continent. My uncle, a strong, supportive
figure during most of my life, had encouraged her to do this,
and they paid most of the expenses incurred.

Within days of our return to England, the legal documents
started coming. My husband, with no thought of reconciliation, was at last pressing for divorce. With the documents
came the news that the other woman was still very much in his
life—they were living together. When I learned this, I ceased
to think about the possibility of reconciliation and, instead,

moved quickly toward the cold reality of divorce.

When the date of our court appearance was finally set, I had one week to prepare for the return trip to the United States. Bob and Judy agreed to care for the girls during my absence, friends helped me move our belongings from the flat to a larger house, and I tried to prepare the girls for the next event in our lives.

Although they had not seen their father for one year, the children were saddened by the news that the reconciliation we all had hoped for would never come. Kathryn, in particular, took the news hard. She grieved, and during one evening became inconsolable. Weeping, she said that she missed her father, that she did not want her parents to get a divorce, that she wanted us all to live together again in a family. I was surprised at the depth of her grief, especially since she had not seen her father for such a long time. Since I, too, was hard pressed to deal with the finality of divorce, I comforted her as best I could, but nothing seemed to help. Fortunately, God sent us marvelous help in the form of Katie.

At our lowest moment, Katie knocked at our door. When I admitted her, she sized up the situation and took over. She told Kathryn that, yes, it was sad that her mother and father were getting a divorce, but her parents still loved her. Moreover, lots of people at L'Abri loved her and Lynn, and while Mommy was away in America, lots of nice things had been planned for them. Katie asked if Lynn and Kathryn would like to come over and watch telly with John and Michael. Both girls were pleased with the prospect of a visit to Katie's. So in a brief time Katie had comforted all three of us. How grateful I was for the care we received on that occasion from a fellow Christian.

As I prepared to leave England, friends prayed with me, some gave me money, since funds were limited, and all gave moral support. I knew that we would be prayed for during the church service on Sunday. Thomas was also an object of prayer. During the time when I could not ask God to care for him, the church could, and many loving prayers were offered in his behalf. And so, as I boarded a plane to fly to America, I felt some inner desolation, but at the same time much comfort, coming toward me from this Christian community.

What an incredibly lonely experience it is to fly to a strange city where one's husband lives with someone else. I knew no one in this city and was hundreds of miles from any friends or family. God did not, however, leave me bereft. For one thing, He had carefully chosen my lawyer. When I left the baggage area in the airport, I was met by my lawyer, a man I had never seen before and had only conversed with once over the phone.

Peter was articulate and friendly. Before he left me at the hotel, he invited me to come for dinner the next night to meet his wife. As I fell into bed, exhausted after three months of anxiety and a transatlantic flight, I knew that God was caring for my human needs in a special way.

During the days that followed, Peter gave me much emotional support and, at the same time, allayed my fears about the loss of custody. I had a delightful evening in his home, talked about L'Abri, and, after the divorce, was taken to the airport by his wife. We had good, open conversations, and I remember these people with fondness.

Those warm, human contacts with Peter and his wife helped to offset the pain of that time. When I saw Thomas for the first time in his lawyer's office, however, all the pain and anger rushed in. It was apparent that there was much unsettled business between us and that now we would never resolve our difficulties. We would simply dissolve the union and go our separate ways.

By the time we saw each other again in the courtroom, my anger had been replaced with a profound sadness. The judge was old and bored by the whole procedure and nearly fell asleep at one point. I was surrounded by strangers, and the only human warmth coming my way was not coming from the man I had slept with for nearly seven years, who had been present at the birth of each of our children, who had comforted me and encouraged me to grow intellectually. It came from a lawyer I hardly knew.

I wept. As I remembered all those who had come to celebrate our wedding, I longed for some friends to come and mourn our divorce. Little ceremony existed to end the sad union. While we had been pronounced man and wife at a happier, earlier time, no one pronounced us divorced. It just happened—casually.

I was awarded a divorce on the grounds of incompatibility, was given custody of the children, and the judge allotted me a small sum in the form of temporary alimony. The children were granted modest support allotments. The support was, of course, figured on the basis of Thomas's limited salary as a doctor in the Public Health Service, and I knew that if the children were to have any share of his future income as a physician in practice, we might need to come to court again. Thus, at a time of profound sadness I had to deal with my own anger about a limited financial settlement.

I was not particularly happy about the grounds for our divorce. Since I believe that all people are more or less incompatible after twenty-four hours of life together, it was hard to handle the concept that so many years of marriage could be wiped out because Thomas and I were merely incompatible. It would have been far more honest to say that the marriage was dissolved because the participants refused to, or were unable to, live together in love.

While the first act of our marriage had been to take communion before God and His witnesses, the first act of our divorce was to sit in the empty courtroom and weep. Thomas sat on one side of the room, crying quietly, and I sat on the other. We were waiting for our lawyers to work out some of the specific provisions of our divorce. As we waited, Thomas said quietly, "Our divorce is a tragedy." I did not ask him what he meant, nor did I know what to say to this man. What was there to say? As the moments passed, I did ask him one question.

The girls often asked me if their Daddy loved me at the time each was born. I could always give Kathryn an affirmative answer, but I did not know what to tell Lynn. She had been conceived during the horrendous year of Thomas's internship. "Tell them both yes," Thomas said. We shared a cup of coffee, and somehow that one act made the whole ordeal more exquisitely painful. That small kindness harked back to an earlier era, and was out of place after all the ripping and tearing of the last years.

When the formalities were over, Thomas rose to go. He was calm and deliberate and headed for a phone, possibly to call Linda and tell her that he was, at last, a free man. I watched him go, feeling empty inside.

As I left the building where my only marriage had been severed, I wondered if the wounds would ever heal. Would I ever be able to see this man at another time and place and feel indifference? When would I stop thinking about Thomas each time I saw a tall man with brown hair? The day did come years later, but when that happened I was a different woman and Thomas was a different man.

As my plane left that city, I felt physically lighter. A heavy weight had been left behind in the courtroom. I was able to accept my divorce and changed status and, even on the plane, feel some joy, some anticipation about a new life.

The legal divorce was a significant ritual in my life. For two whole years I had bombarded heaven with prayers for reconciliation, and had encouraged many other Christians to join me in my supplications. But when the time came to obtain the divorce, I was able to accept the inevitable and emerge feeling genuinely free.

I believe this was due, in part, to the two-year waiting period before the divorce. Although most people favor speedy divorces once one of the parties decides to end the union, I am grateful that Thomas did not press for divorce earlier. During that time I had space to recover from the pain of the early separation and seek healing inside a therapeutic community. I had time to begin to rebuild my life as a single person. When the divorce finally came, I was ready for it emotionally.

I left the city believing that our marriage was irrevocably

over. It had finally been accorded a funeral, and there were two witnesses, Thomas and I. I cherished no longings that he would ever come back, should his second marriage fail. Divorce is serious business. While some people seem to view it as an interim act between marriage and remarriage to the same person, for me, divorce marked the absolute end for my first and only marriage.

I have been appalled at the number of women I have met in my travels who hope their former husbands will come back, even after these men remarry. Sad and waiting, these Christian women hold their lives in abeyance while at the same time hoping that their husbands' second marriages will fail. I do not believe this is good, nor do I believe that it is biblical. For Mosaic Law recognized the divorced person's right to remarry any person except the person he divorced. According to Dwight H. Small in *The Right to Remarry*, "The Mosaic divorce bill was called by the Jews 'A Bill of Cutting Off.' There was never any question but what Judaism meant complete dissolution." Thus, while I had hoped for reconciliation throughout a long period of separation, I entertained no thought of remarriage to Thomas after our divorce.

Since the judge had ordered us back to the continental United States so that the girls could be raised on American soil, I faced the prospect of leaving L'Abri permanently in another nine months. That thought saddened me, but I accepted it as part of God's plan for us. I planned to enjoy those last months in England and make concrete plans for a return to America. I had no idea where we would settle.

For the remainder of the two weeks in America, I visited friends and family in various cities. Everywhere I went I found concern and expressed love. When depression finally hit during the last days of the sojourn, I was at my sister's home, and I was able to tell her how I felt. She and I have always been soul mates. I found the Holy Spirit especially close during those days. It was as if He hovered, saying gently, "Don't worry, Brenda. Your life is at a new beginning. I have a good future planned for you."

11

Return to America

Then into His hand went mine,
And into my heart came He;
And I walk in a light divine
The path I had feared to see.
GEORGE MACDONALD

As I flew back to London after the divorce, I slumped in the seat, profoundly tired. Behind me were three long years of apprehension and waiting. Before me was an unknown future. I marveled that my body had apparently withstood so much strain, for I had been quite healthy during the whole ordeal. But my face looked older and haggard. As the plane droned on, I felt my whole body begin to relax. How wonderful, I thought, not to get any more horrible documents from lawyers. All that summer one fat envelope after another had arrived, destroying my peace. And how good to face a new beginning. As I stared out of the airplane window at the clouds and ocean below, I asked God for a time of respite and quiet.

I needed some time to plan for our return to America. The judge had given me until the thirtieth of June to bring the children back into the country. I did not know where we three would settle, and the thought of packing up again to move for the third time in three years unnerved me. So I pushed the thought into some dark corner. In time I would examine the problem, but now I longed for some simplicity in life. I wanted to sew, bake bread, attend some plays, and talk with friends. God had given us a gift—nine months to consolidate friendships, travel, and enjoy England—and I wanted to spend them well.

These months enabled me to make the transition into a new phase of life as a divorced woman. At last I had time to enjoy the friends who had gone through the trauma and crisis with me. Gretchen gave me theater tickets for my birthday that year, and she and I went to plays together. Mardi and I went for walks occasionally in the park behind Ros's flat. That Easter, Ros and I flew to Switzerland with the children to visit friends at L'Abri.

Interspersed with all these good hours were other times, when I prayed and asked God where the three of us should live once we returned to America. I could not bear the thought of once more being alone in some American city, knowing no one and raising the girls completely without help. I was not close to my family, and so I never considered living near them. But where to go? And what to do? I did not feel that I would be able to find a teaching job and was not sure I wanted to teach. Frankly, I was thirty-one and did not know what I wanted to do with my life.

During this last year, God sent a new couple to the church. John was a doctor, who came to England to study at the University of London and participate in the life of the L'Abri church. Penny, his sunny wife, had worked as a nurse before the births of Matt and Luke. They moved into a house nearby, and so we three often rode to church with them. Although still prejudiced against medicine and doctors, I liked John, and Penny became my confidante in time.

When they later learned that I must return to America and that I did not know where I would go, they asked me to come to Seattle and live near them. I was touched by their offer of friendship, and during the months that followed, I considered it more seriously. They told me that they would give us whatever help we needed in relocating, and John even offered financial help. Since we needed family and continuity in our lives, I decided to accept their offer. So Penny and I bought our trunks, carted them home in their red Volvo, and prepared to move two families to Seattle.

Knowing that we would live near John and Penny made it somewhat easier to leave the community behind. We had internalized their love and acceptance, and we felt better about life. But it was wrenching to once more pack up a life—the best I had ever known—and get ready to start out all over again.

Some fifteen friends came to share a meal the last week we were in London. As they left, these friends took my carpet, lamp, books—the things I would not send to our new life. This time it was not painful to watch my furniture carted out the door, and I noted this with no small pleasure. I was happy to have something to give to those who had given so much to us.

When we finally drove to the airport, we were not alone. Many came to bid us farewell. Katie and Barney were there, Ros, Mardi, Gretchen, Susie, and Will. When Lynn lost her favorite doll in the hubbub and let out a howl, Gretchen saved the day by going to an airport shop and paying a small fortune for a replacement. What a contrast our leave-taking was to our arrival. Less than two years before, I had landed in Heathrow with two bewildered children in tow and had carried our luggage through the airport without any help. Yet here we were now, surrounded by good friends who had shown, in countless ways, that they had an investment in our lives.

Only when we left the friends behind and went forward to the boarding area did desolation sweep over me. Why was God sending us away from this community which had given us so much? Didn't He know that I was still a woman alone and that we needed to be part of an ongoing Christian community? At that time I felt John, Penny, and I were too small a unit to function as a community.

We boarded the plane, found our seats, and I pushed my grief aside momentarily. I had yet another problem to deal with. For the first time the children would be leaving me, to go to their father for two long months. Only four and six, both were apprehensive about the pending visit. They had not seen Thomas for two years and did not know the woman he had married. Lynn, in particular, was gloomy about the prospect. I feel now that she was too young to be separated from me. In contrast, Kathryn, who was six, was much more eager to go to her father.

We flew to my former mother-in-law's house. Not only did I need to ship our few belongings, long since stored in her attic, to Seattle, but Thomas and I had planned to exchange the children in her home. I decided to leave a few hours before he arrived, simply because I felt it would be easier on the children and I did not want to see him. In total we spent about a week with his mother. It was perhaps unwise: I was tense and full of sadness; she was concerned. It was not a happy time for anyone.

My children had been exposed to a short, biweekly visitation pattern during the first year of the separation. Now they would experience another visitation schedule, the once-yearly longer visit. Neither is without significant pain. Those short biweekly visits had conjured up great longing in Kathryn for her father's ongoing presence. They had perpetuated unhealthy patterns of interaction between us, her parents, and it had been harder for Thomas and me to get inwardly free of each other. While the once-yearly visit obviously cuts down on parental interaction and enables the children to develop a stronger sense of home, it taxes them deeply.

I still remember the day I left them at my mother-in-law's to await Thomas's arrival. The children had awakened at 5:00 A.M. because of jet lag. Hearing their soft voices, I left my bedroom, to tell them to come join me for a cuddle. When we were once more in bed, and their little bodies pressed close, they were full of questions. They whispered, "Who will comfort us at our daddy's when you're not there? What will we do when we miss you?" Kathryn wondered what Linda would be like; Lynn muttered that she did not want to have her mommy leave.

As best I could, I assured them that their father would be with them during nonworking hours. I also said that since I would not be there to care for them, they should learn to comfort each other. The summer would draw them closer together. They admitted that they were relieved not to have to go alone. I added that I would write often, pray a lot, and send frequent little presents.

In truth, I felt absolutely impotent. When I left hours later, I had given my children all I could—some fragile promises. That first leave-taking was one of the hardest of my life's experiences. I felt that, while their father had a right and a need to see them, his right was not satisfied without some cost to the girls. These small children were asked to leave the one person they knew best to visit a man they scarcely knew and his unknown wife. If they needed a mother, they would have to supply this need in some other fashion or go without.

I had no way to gauge the long-term effects of this maternal deprivation, and knew it would do little good to try, anyway. The courts had established the visitation pattern at Thomas's request, and anything I, as mother, would ever say would be suspect. The custodial parent can say little about the deleterious effects of visitation, lest she be accused of planting negative thoughts in her children's minds. This well-understood accusation effectively silences any remonstrances. Yet who knows the children better than a caring, sensitive custodial parent?

I knew that I could defend my children in almost any other arena of life except this area of visitation. Since their father was educated, decent, would not neglect or abuse them, and had a right to seasonal and reasonable visitation, I could do nothing, except to let them go—to fend for themselves in the territory of his second marriage.

As I prepared to leave my young children, I hoped that someday the courts would reexamine the whole area of visitation, putting the emphasis on the child's needs, rather than either parent's right to a slice of the child's life. Should a preschool child be required to leave his home and custodial parent for two months each year? Should an adolescent be re-

quired to visit the noncustodial parent if the child does not
wish to go?

Much is required of children of divorce in this travel between two alien and sometimes hostile worlds. Some leave
one world for the other, and, in so doing, grow to adulthood
with their feet either planted firmly in the two worlds or both
feet in neither. Others, because of internal pressure, choose
one world and gradually reject the other. It is impossible to
weigh the benefits of visitation or tabulate the losses in terms
of personal security and loneliness. Whatever its impact, visitation is, at its best and worst, a constant reminder that a home
once intact has been divided.

Thus, as I left my children and flew away on yet another
airplane, I was glad I was a Christian. At that time I did all I
could do: I placed those two children in God's hands, and
acknowledged that I did not possess them, but had been given
them to raise. For an interval I could do nothing to bind up
their hurts, to give them love and care. I prayed that Thomas
would be attentive and that Linda would treat them well. And,
finally, I asked the Holy Spirit to supply any comfort that my
small daughters might need.

After I prayed, some tranquility came. But I did not realize
how bereft I was until I spent several days with my Aunt Stella
and Uncle Blake in Florida. As I walked the beach alone and
listened to the ocean, the inner grief was eased and ebbed
away. I missed my L'Abri friends. I missed my children. But
the Holy Spirit ministered to me, and as the sun tanned my
body, I discovered that a part of my personality began to surface that had been buried for years.

No longer the resident, twenty-four-hour parent, I became
Brenda again, for the first time since I left college. Marriage
had been constricting rather than freeing during the final
years, and single parenthood carried heavy responsibilities.
Thus, during those early days in the sun, I shed some cumber-
some garments which I had worn for a long time.

After this brief time of renewal, I flew to Seattle to create yet another life. Ros had given me the name of good friends, the Burnetts, and so I was able to stay with this family for several weeks as I looked for a house. John and Penny had already bought a home, and I knew I wanted to live near them. I believed that physical proximity was essential for the maintenance of any kind of close relationship.

During this period of my life, God was very much there. He led me to the small frame house with a fireplace, white walls, and gold carpet that I recognized instantly as our home. Unlike the other house at 16 Burnham Way, this little house beckoned and promised peace and safety. I was pleased to discover that I had just enough money to assume the loan after I purchased a car and some furniture, and so I, a divorced woman without a job, without established credit, was able to circumvent the banks and their rigorous credit checks.

And as a link with the past, Barney came to Seattle to film a television program weeks before the children returned from their visit, and he stayed with John and Penny. During his stay, he put up bookshelves for me in my new house. He had often repaired things in London, and so it was heartwarming to see him at work with hammer and screwdriver. In time both he and Katie came to see us for three weeks. Their visit meant so much to me. They and I were members of the same family—God's. How good it was to have this continuity in our lives, this continuing bond with L'Abri. I knew God had sent them, in part to ease our transition into a new life; we did not feel so cut off from the recent past.

Possessor once again of worldly goods, I was soon ready to tackle an immediate problem. I needed to find a job. For weeks prior to the children's homecoming, I rode around Seattle looking for employment—without success. In time—at the right time—I found more than a job. I found a new career as a writer and editor, and in addition, I tackled once again the whole problem of the working mother.

12

Career and the Working Mother

We have almost stopped being a caring society
that cares for others. We seem to be hesitant about
making a commitment to anyone or anything, including our own flesh and blood.

URIE BRONFENBRENNER

Most people approach the subject of the working mother
from the mother's point of view. They point out, and with
reason, that it is wasteful for an educated, restless, ambitious
woman to funnel all of her energies into her role as mother and
keeper of the home. If she does, she may eventually turn to
bridge or alcohol and end up with poor mental health. One has
only to read what Jesse Bernard says in *The Future of Marriage* about the mental health of housewives as it compares
with the general populace to become alarmed.

For a moment, I would like to examine the issue of the
working mother from a child's point of view. Imagine a child
growing up alone in a single-parent household. The father,
young and intelligent, was drowned when this child was two
years old, and her baby sister was a mere two months. He left
behind an insurance policy of five hundred dollars, his total
monetary legacy to his young widow.

The father had been the college student; his widow had not
finished high school. So she took a series of low-paying jobs to
support herself and the child. The widow gave the baby to her
mother-in-law to raise. She said that the baby-sitter had been
negligent and allowed the baby to get badly burned when she
crawled next to the stove. Since the young widow felt her baby
needed better care, and since she simply could not work and

cope with two small children, the young mother gave her baby up. She said later that this was one of the heartbreaks of her life.

Times were hard, and after a number of jobs as a store clerk, the widow finally became a telephone operator. During her seven-year stint as an operator, the mother had to work split shifts, and finding it difficult to secure child care, on occasion was forced to leave her nine-year-old alone, sometimes until nine or ten o'clock at night. The child grew accustomed to eating an indifferent meal at an indifferent neighbor's house when her mother worked late. And she nearly always returned home after school to an empty house.

As the child grew older in this life of poverty with her mother, she grew accustomed to loneliness. The hardest times were dusk and late evening on those days when her mother worked late. The child ached when she saw the neighborhood fathers return home at day's end, while she remained alone in the empty house. But dusk could not compare with the terrors of late evening. Then the child sat transfixed with fear in the middle of the living room floor, looking through the adjoining bedroom and kitchen and beyond to the hooked screen door, praying that no burglar would come to her door.

The mother was not indifferent to her child's need. Indeed, the mother prayed often for the safety of her child and worried incessantly about her welfare. It was just that she was trapped in poverty, and she was, in some ways, defeated by life. The mother did the best she could. How often during those seven years of split shifts the mother walked (they had no car) the one and a half miles home to see her daughter in the middle of the day. Those were the good days, which found the child sitting on the curb kicking dirt as she waited to see her mother at the foot of the hill.

I was the child of that working mother, and I remember much of childhood as a series of lonely, empty days. Granted, I grew up quickly and became independent as I cared for myself, but in essence I grew up alone. When my mother was there, she was tired and had much to do. Saturdays she did her food shopping; Sundays she cleaned our apartment and napped. She had precious little time to devote to the arduous task of child rearing. In addition, she did not have the stamina. When we had any contest of wills, I generally won because I had more energy. Thus I grew up with little respect for authority.

The salvation of my life and my psyche lay in the frequent vacations with my grandparents on their dairy farm. On these occasions the unremitting loneliness and sterility of life with Mother abated, and I was literally lost in the warm nurture of an extended family that consisted of an unmarried aunt and uncle, grandparents, and, best of all, a sister who was my boon companion.

The best gift of my childhood was given to me by my grandparents, in the form of companionship. Granddaddy, in particular, was accessible. No matter what task he needed to perform, I could go along. As we toured North Carolina in his 1950 Ford, I learned about politics (he read the *Congressional Record* every day), FDR, the Depression, the courtship of Granny and, best of all, about Granddaddy himself. He shared himself with me, and in so doing he taught me values, helped form my character, ambitions, and belief in the eternal verities. Without Granddaddy's love, I might not have survived the vicissitudes of life.

Then why did I have such a hard time at first, giving my children the place they deserved in my life? Life with Mother had taught me that I did not want my children to return home after school to an empty house, to have an indifferent, passive baby-sitter, to cry out for intellectual stimulation. On the other hand, my attractive mother cared for me, and she provided a model of chastity as a woman alone.

And from my good-natured grandfather I received what is golden to a child—time and companionship. Because of him I knew that if I ever expected to impact the lives of my children, I would need to spend much time with them, teaching them, loving and enjoying them.

I was unable, at first, to give my children what they needed, because I had bought the cultural sell. I was deeply influenced by Betty Friedan's *The Feminine Mystique* and felt that I was wasting my mind, life, and talents by staying home with my small children.

I heard the slogan that sums up much of the modern-day approach to parenting—"It is quality and not quantity that counts"—and I believed it. It was natural to go to work and was unnatural to stay home. I never identified with women who lost themselves in the diaper pail or in play with their children. Unschooled for parenting, it was more natural for me to teach a college class than to spend a complete day with my baby. Women who spent hours playing bridge or attending garden clubs were beyond my ken. So, too, were women who engaged in volunteerism. Why not get paid for skills, rather than let schools or hospitals exploit them? And so, I worked during the infancies of both daughters.

When God became more real to me, however, I began to see all of life—and my role as a mother—differently. I examined the cultural attitudes which state that we must seek self-fulfillment before all else. At base, this is an irresponsible and selfish concept. It does not take into account the fact that other lives and psyches may depend upon us.

According to the culture, children may be impediments to self-fulfillment, to personal growth, to fun. But the Christian views children in a different light: They are gifts from God, to be taught and nurtured. As gifts, they are a high responsibility.

When we become single parents, we are, in essence, all that our young children have, particularly at first. While the father may send a support check, the divorced mother is the twenty-four-hour parent, seven days a week. This is a heavy responsibility. In a real sense, our children's humanity is dependent on our choices and parenting skills.

One of the great dangers in being a parent is that we will

unwittingly neglect our children. What is neglect? W. Hugh Missildine, in *Your Inner Child of the Past,* says:

> Neglect is usually a parental attitude often expressed as preoccupation with work or "duties" which results in the parent having little time for, interest in or awareness of the child's need for a continuing attachment with an adult to whom he can turn for help in satisfying his needs.

What does neglect feel like to the child? Having experienced neglect in life with my mother, I know that one feels empty, frightened, essentially alone in the universe. One is trapped in a small, constricted world of worries and fears; no one comes to listen and to find out who you are. Read about Winston Churchill's early life, and you will discover what neglect felt like to a sensitive and intelligent boy. Although Churchill had rich and famous parents, he felt that his mother was like a "distant star." He loved her, he idolized her, and eventually he actually implored her to spend time with him and take a deeper interest in his life. But his mother was too preoccupied with her own life to give young Winston what he needed.

In an article in *Scientific American* (August, 1972), Urie Bronfenbrenner writes about the trend in the American family toward disorganization. His thesis is thatnthe origins of this alienation are to be found in the child's lack of contact with the adult world. Not only are parents gone a good deal of the time, leaving children with passive baby-sitters, but children are isolated from other adults, as well. He refers to a study of middle-class fathers who told interviewers that they spent an average of 15–20 minutes with their infants daily. When the father's voice was actually recorded, by attaching a microphone to the infant's shirt, it was discovered that, in reality, these fathers spent only 37.7 seconds per day interacting with their youngsters.

As Christians, we must not neglect our children, for in so

doing we send them into life impoverished. Further, since we as parents are God to the young child, we instill, through neglect, the feeling that not even He is finally concerned about their needs. It is hard for the neglected child to grow up and believe that God is intimately concerned about the details of his life.

As single parents and Christians we need a rich, warm relationship with each child. Before we consider the question of a job, we must first come to terms with our children's place in our lives. And work falls into a manageable place once our priorities are right.

When I returned to America, I clearly needed money and had to go to work. But my young children needed me. Thus, I encountered a dilemma. How could I reenter the work force and at the same time adequately parent my children? This is the question that most divorced mothers face today, since few can afford to stay at home. Fortunately, I was divorced in a state that still granted alimony to women, and the judge awarded me a modest amount for a three-year period. I have been additionally fortunate that Thomas has paid both alimony and child support regularly. Thus, I had a modest income and could entertain the prospect of a part-time job.

This is not the case with many women today. Influenced by the feminist philosophy, many women are not seeking adequate financial provision from their estranged husbands. And judges seldom award alimony. Even when support is established, many irresponsible fathers refuse to pay. This means that most divorced women have the difficult task of earning enough money to support themselves and their children. Hence, the 1976 September issue of *McCall's* terms divorced women and their children "the new poor."

Sometimes I wonder if the women who forgo child support, and the judges who refuse to award even temporary alimony to mothers, have any idea just how demanding a full-time job can be for the single parent. A job that requires eight hours in truth exacts nine or ten when one adds dressing time, commuting time, and the end-of-the-day reentry time. Thus, a working mother spends from 7:30 A.M. to 6 P.M. on her job if she works 9–5. Children and their needs must be sandwiched in at early dawn and early evening.

Such a parent misses out on two critical times of the day with her children. When a woman leaves for work before school, the children must get lunches packed, get themselves off to school, and bear the responsibility for locking up the house. Most important, the children miss out on a mother's love and care during that critical hour. And after school? There is no mother to listen to the joys and woes of the day or to supervise the older child's activities. So children fend for themselves and handle their own emotional needs. Or do they?

It is all very well to insist that quality time is all children really need, but when do they get it? How many single parents greet the dawn to have intimate times with their youngsters? And after work, what about quality time? Most divorced women who work full time tell me about arriving home, tired and hungry, only to be greeted by disgruntled children, an untidy house, and unmet needs.

Weekend time could be quality time if food shopping, laundry, and house cleaning did not remain to be done. And what about the parent's social and emotional needs? Many look to the weekend to ski, date, and spend time with friends. I asked one little girl how often she talked with her working mother. "Seldom," was her reply. She went on to say that when her mother returned from work at the end of the day, she called her friends, fixed supper, and promised to read a story—if there was time. There apparently never was.

For the divorced mother, I would suggest that a full-time job is not the only viable option, even when funds are low. When faced with economic need, most women probably feel that they have little freedom of choice. They either work full time, and let their children fend for themselves, or the family starves. Also, many women like to work full time. They enjoy the money, the status, and the freedom from their children. But it is extremely difficult to be an effective parent during the hours of life that are left.

There are other options available to the divorced mother who must work. If she is a Christian, she can trust God. I am convinced that when we give our children the place they need in our lives, God takes care of our financial situation. Or a woman can attempt to have her ex-husband pay adequate child support. Additionally, a divorced woman may move in with another divorced mother and share expenses. If a woman is fortunate, she may receive some help in the area of child care from an extended family of fellow Christians.

When I became a working mother the second time, I met a lawyer who suggested that I start my own business as an editorial consultant and work out of my own home. I could thus work during school hours and evenings, could deduct a portion of my mortgage payment as a business expense (under tax laws at that time), and could, by charging an hourly fee, earn as much in three hours as I had formerly earned during a full day of teaching.

I found it comparatively easy to thus begin a new career that fitted into my life. I did not have to distort our family life for my career. In the beginning I edited a quarterly journal for lawyers and judges, then because of referrals, I acted as a consultant for the criminal-justice task force on drug abuse. In time I signed a year's contract to edit a monthly newsletter for a group of economists, and at the same time I wrote for other businesses.

Two months after I had arrived in Seattle, knowing no one outside of John and Penny, I was launched in an interesting new career. Moreover, I discovered that I enjoyed this career as much as I had enjoyed teaching and I was, at last, able to write.

I had been writing since I entered grade school; poems and essays that were stuffed in boxes and drawers. As a college teacher I had taught freshmen how to write. But I had never published and was too timid to believe I ever could. When I started editing, it was fun to see articles that I had written in print. One of the first articles that I wrote, an essay on alcoholism, later won a second prize in a writer's conference, and during the first year of editing, I published an article on Christian community in a local magazine.

I discovered that in having my own business I had great flexibility. I could take time off if the children were ill, could work evenings to meet deadlines, could take a week off and drive the three of us to San Francisco between publications. Never had I enjoyed such freedom in any previous job.

In addition to freedom and flexibility, this new career was God-given and as such, was tailored to my needs and abilities. God knew that I was a divorced mother who needed a job. He also knew me and knew what would best develop my talents and meet my needs as a person. Once I made the decision to trust Him and to provide good care for my children, at whatever personal cost, the career came as a matter of course. It did not spring full-blown from my brain: I would never have had the courage to believe that I could function as an editor (I had never worked as an editor) and earn enough money to supplement the check Thomas sent. But God knew.

And even if one is left destitute and must work full time, what then? I watched a neighbor handle this problem. Her husband disappeared and left her and their three children without any money. My neighbor, a Christian, appeared at my door one day, ostensibly to return one of our wandering kittens. Although I had never talked to Jane before, within a few moments she was sharing the circumstances of her life. And as months passed I watched God care for her. First, checks mysteriously arrived to fund her family's needs. Then within a few weeks Jane found a modest job. Today she provides braces, lessons—many of the accoutrements of the middle-class life— for her children and maintains a home on a bookkeeper's salary. Of course, God supplements her income from time to time.

I watched, somewhat amazed at the quality of care God provided for Jane and her family. Once the wind blew down her old fence in the backyard and within a short time, the neighbor who shared the fence had replaced it, at no cost to Jane. On another occasion, Jane needed a new car and a relative gave her an impressive Dodge Dart.

Jane's life as a single parent has contained hard struggles, particularly in the area of parenting. Since she worked full time, Jane mentioned feeling exhausted at day's end. She felt there were just too many demands on her time and too many needs waiting to be met. But she grappled with the problem of too little time, curtailed her social life until she had improved her parenting skills, and concentrated on the relationship with her three children. As she felt better about herself as a parent, as she dealt with all areas of her life more responsibly, Jane began to feel better about herself as a person.

For the divorced woman who must secure employment and at the same time raise her children, life will never be rich if she neglects her children. I remember what one man said to me: "Most divorced women will ultimately get themselves together, even if it takes some a long time. But when I meet a divorced woman who obviously knows who she is, I am only half impressed. I want to see her children."

Scripture enjoins us to concentrate on the right priorities, and economic need is not the highest priority for a Christian. Even if we find ourselves without money, we must still ask what are our high responsibilities before God. And, after a relationship with God, comes our relationship with our family, in this case our children. What happens when we stare fear in the face and refuse to be internally destroyed? When we give our children the time and interest they need, we see them unfold and become beautiful people. I am continually surprised and gratified at the wholeness of my two daughters. What is more, I feel good about the choices I have made.

13
Men, Women, and Sex

Today what matters most for many people is their growth and happiness, their own fulfillment, doing their own thing . . . . We seem to be sunk in individualism.

URIE BRONFENBRENNER

When I returned to America after two years in London, I discovered that a major concern during the next phase of my life would be the whole area of men and sex. I was thirty-two and had fairly demanding sexual needs; what is more, I was ready to be a warm, loving woman for some fortunate man. Having known English men for those two years, I found that American men, who are far more direct and aggressive, looked quite appealing.

Why wasn't sex a major problem at L'Abri? There were several reasons. First, I was still eager to be reconciled with my husband for one of those years. It was simply not possible to desire reconciliation and at the same time actively pursue an involvement with another man. Granted, there were several casual dating relationships with men (two of whom were American doctors), but no relationship of any depth formed. Secondly, I was in a loving community of Christians who shared the same values that I subscribed to, among them the virtue of chastity. One should never minimize the impact of a caring community or a shared value system. I did not have to go to bed with a man in order to feel someone's arms around me or to know that I was a significant person. Sadly, some have admitted that they engage in casual sex because that is the

115

only way they can be touched by another human being.

Moreover, the attractive men at L'Abri were either married or a good deal younger than I was. In addition, while I longed for a relationship with a man, I knew I was not ready for one. Friends encouraged me to put my life in order and allow time for the wounds to heal before I complicated my life with a man, or men.

But when I stepped off the plane in America, I sensed that the time had come to deal with this aspect of the single life. I began to be bombarded with the "modern" values concerning sex, and I met an attractive American male. Thus, I began to sort out rather quickly what I, a divorced woman and a Christian, believed to be true in the sexual area.

Everything I read heralded the glory of the new sexual revolution. Singles bars were in their genesis, and they facilitated what some call the "meat-market experience," with its predatory rituals that lead to casual sex. Although the word *chastity* was never mentioned, the culture, by the very absence of the term, indicated that chastity had either gone underground or was possibly an extinct virtue.

The current view was that casual sex—any kind of sexual union— was distinctively healthy. Intimidated by the cultural sexual sell, I encountered the mentality C. S. Lewis describes in *Mere Christianity:*

> In the first place our warped nature, the devils who tempt us, and all the contemporary propaganda for lust, combine to make us feel that the desires we are resisting are so "natural," so "healthy" and so reasonable, that it is almost perverse and abnormal to resist them.

To attempt chastity, I saw, was to risk becoming a cultural anomaly. Who else was attempting the medieval virtue? Moreover, the culture indicated that a female celibate, unless she was religious, must be a frigid, man-hating woman. Since I did not want to be viewed as man hating, I thought that surely I, a Christian, would find support and encouragement in the church.

That was not so. The singles group I attended in one fashionable church seemed to have as its primary goal the pairing off of men and women. Any Christianity was tacked on, or superficial. Ministers told me that all the divorced people they knew were sleeping around. "Even Christian divorced people?" I countered. "Even Christians," some said with a bit of sadness. I soon learned from these particular conversations that neither God nor the Protestant Church expected the divorced to abstain from sexual intercourse. It would apparently be inhuman to try.

One well-meaning minister even gave me absolution before the fact when I went to him to discuss the conflicts I was having as a Christian woman with sexual needs. I came to see that much of American Christianity is cultural Christianity, and is steeped in moral relativism. It was all right for me to attempt chastity, since I had a sensitive conscience, but many of God's representatives did not expect their divorced parishioners to do anything but satisfy their sexual needs. Fortunately, this was not the kind of Christianity I had encountered at L'Abri, where people felt that if a Christian were enjoined to do something, then with the power of the Holy Spirit and the encouragement of the Christian community, he should at least try.

Much later I did meet a minister who talked with me about the battered people who showed up in his office for counseling—most of whom spoke of the joys of sex in curiously joyless tones. And I later heard about other Christians who found support for biblical sexual morality within their churches. But this supportive mentality was more apparent in churches in the Southeast than in those churches I attended in the Seattle area. That I found little support from Protestant ministers in the area of sexual morality I note with sadness, not condemnation.

Thus, I saw that my struggle would be essentially a lonely one as I attempted to work out a response to the pressures of my new life. God had, however, provided a survival unit in the form of my friend Penny. She, as half of my Seattle family, was a source of encouragement and good fun. I saw Penny almost daily, and she listened as I voiced my needs. Penny, warmly human, invariably mirrored the Christian perspective to me in her responses. There was much sharing and much laughter in those four o'clock teas. I owe a lot to my friend Penny.

As I began a new career as an editor, I met numerous men and was occasionally propositioned by the married and the unmarried alike. As I was propositioned, I started to form a view of sexuality that is both pragmatic and Christian. I listened to the people in front of me, educated men and women, who were engaging in open marriages or open sexuality, and I collected data: I wanted to see if the new sexual freedom worked for them.

I met several men who told me that they practiced open marriage; i.e., that they were having affairs. They spoke openly of their sexual exploits and of the "maturity" with which their wives handled their affairs. In each case, the wife had begun having affairs after she had discovered her husband's infidelity.

One man had wistful eyes and an exhausted quality about his face. Another was incredulous when I told him that I was struggling to be a Christian in the sexual area. He, married then, said, "I embrace what you call immoral experiences." He went on to say with some degree of longing, "The trouble with you Christians is that you water down the Bible, thinking that you will win people like me for your cause. Someday I would like to have a long talk with Christians who take the Bible seriously."

In addition to the various men I met, I started to meet educated, divorced women in situations similar to mine. Most had children and were engaged in some sort of profession. I found that many had begun having sexual encounters during their teens, and they did not see the point in saying no to their sexual instinct. Granted, I met a few women who were attempting to lead moral lives, but, in the main, I discovered that most had imbibed the cultural view of sexuality; i.e., that the mere presence of their sexual instinct indicated that it must be satisfied.

As I met these divorced women, I eventually met their children. I discovered, I am sad to say, an amazing lack of concern on the part of many women for the needs of their children. Not only did they leave the children for a full-time job (most felt they had to), but many left their children evenings and weekends, as well. One question that I asked the women was what they did with their children when they slept with men. Few left their homes. Although the women had used discretion at the outset, it soon became logistically impossible, or so they said, to always go away in order to go to bed with a man. So most engaged in intercourse while their children slept in a nearby room.

Some had lovers move in with them, and a few had numerous live-in boyfriends over the course of several years. When I queried the women about the possible impact on their children, the response was that the children were fine and liked the new man. This was not the response I obtained from women who had lovers move out after a long time. One mother said that her children were sad when her lover left after their three-year relationship. Could it have been like losing a stepfather or close relative, I wondered? Apparently, few women had contemplated the cost that their children might have to pay, in terms of personal pain, for their mother's liaisons.

I became deeply concerned about children of divorce as I saw what their new life-style was doing to them. A few were seeing therapists because of various problems: Two children had begun to steal; another child had deteriorated markedly in academic performance. I met a few who appeared stable and relatively happy; I met many who appeared lonely and forlorn, particularly during the early time of parental separation. I did not want my own children to be adversely affected by my behavior, and thus I watched the children in front of me carefully.

I wondered how it would affect them over time to have to deal with their mothers' various lovers. What did they think when they stumbled out in the morning to greet a new male face, one they might never see again? And how did they deal with the promises made by the lovers, to take them camping or to teach them various skills in the future? Said one little boy, "X is going to take me sailing next summer." But what if X had been replaced by someone else when summer came? What would this boy feel if he saw X, the maker of promises, go?

Why this insensitivity? Are these mothers intent on deliberately harming their children? I do not believe they think in these terms at all. Many women I have met have simply bought the cultural sexual sell: They believe that their sexual needs have top priority in their lives and that satisfying them is both natural and healthy. In addition, they believe that the chief goal of their lives is to obtain their own personal happiness and fulfillment. All else, including their children, is secondary.

As I met these men and women, I began to see that the highly touted casual sex is a mechanical, gritty process. On one occasion, I went to a singles bar with a friend. As we observed the people there, he explained the predatory process involved. He stated that women who wanted to get picked up came singly or in pairs, and the mating process was thereby easier. The men stood or sat gazing at the available female flesh until some sign, probably a lingering gaze, indicated that the women were interested. Both men and women were clearly predators in that situation, and it was all done according to certain rituals that everyone seemed to know. The whole experience, while sociologically interesting, was humanly appalling.

Said one man whom I dated, "Casual sex is a sordid process. When it gets to be ten-thirty in a bar and you want someone to sleep with, you will take a woman home to bed, knowing that there will never be anything between you except this one-night stand. This knowledge is degrading to both." He continued, "Most who engage in casual sex—and I did—are needy people, who desperately want sexual affirmation. Sometimes, however, they get just the opposite of affirmation from the people they pick up."

As I looked at the lives before me, I concluded that even with clamoring sexual needs, lust would never win me. The people who spoke of the joys of casual sex did not evidence joy. The women admitted that they were at the end of some man's rope—if they cared at all—as they waited for the phone to ring. As I witnessed women struggle to don the mask of independence after each man left their lives, I concluded pragmatically that sex and more sex was not giving the women I met the promised joy. On the contrary, I saw pain and disorder in their lives.

But what about the long-term relationship, that which some men and women hope will grow into love? My psychiatrist had told me years before that sex was inevitable in a relationship of any duration. He implied that something was nonfunctional if a man and a woman failed to have intercourse after the relationship had gone beyond a certain point. While I knew that casual sex had no lure, I felt that I was ready to love another man, and I wondered how my Christian ethics would keep me from a sexual liaison if genuine love were involved.

About this time, I met a man who had a relationship with a woman that lasted for several years. Although the man told the woman in modernese that he wanted honest sex and nothing more, the woman, as some women (and men) will, grew to love this person. What is more, she began to press him for matrimony. In time, he left her and, within a year or so, found someone else to be his wife. And the first woman? Because of the depth of her involvement with this man, it has taken her a long time to put her life back together. Thus, I became cynical about the culturally "honest" long-term, but uncommitted, relationship.

It was not easy to keep men out of my bed. There were times when I was so lonely and in such need that had any man come to my door, I would have succumbed. Fortunately, God knew that and made those times bearable. No man came to my door, but often a good female friend came by, and we had hours of laughter and good conversation. God never leaves us bereft or requires of us more than we, with His help, are able to render.

At one time, however, I seemed cut off from God. When I ended a relationship with a man who wanted honest sex (whatever that is) and little else, I was angry at God and felt there was little comfort in doing the right thing. There is little comfort—at the time. The comfort comes later, and with it comes joy at having said yes to what one knew in one's heart was the right course of action.

When I finally concluded that I did not want a battered life or further scarring for my children, I asked myself what I did want. I wanted in my thirties what I had essentially desired in my twenties: to love and be loved by one man in a committed marital union. This kind of relationship, I felt, would best satisfy my human needs. In the end I had little trouble opting for the quality article as opposed to the counterfeit. I have always hated plastic flowers.

In stating my long-term goal—to love and be loved by one man—I was better able to handle the pressures of the immediate and postpone gratification of my sexual desires. It was not easy. At times, as I did a sorting process through the available men who came my way, I doubted that I would ever find a man whom I would want to marry and, with him, confront the difficulties posed by a second marriage. Sometimes I doubted that God could, or would, give me the rich, deep union that I longed for. And the dark times of doubting were the times when it was hardest to say no to sexual needs.

And what about Christianity? Did I attempt what Lewis calls the "unpopular virtue of chastity" simply because of the joyless lives around me? Hardly. I poured over Romans 7 and 8, read Romans 12 and other passages of Scripture. I looked up all the passages on *chastity, fornication, impurity,* and was chagrined to find no concordance that contained the more common word—"sex."

What I learned was this: That while I subscribed to biblical truths and felt that Christians were enjoined to "flee sexual lusts," precepts alone would never keep me. In the crunch, only the living Person of Christ mattered. At such times I prayed, and the Holy Spirit came to my aid, sometimes in humorous ways and known only to my best friend.

But if we fail—as we all do—to live up to the rigorous standard set for the sons and daughters of God—what then? Then we must ask forgiveness and go on. For as C. S. Lewis says in *Mere Christianity:*

> Very often what God first helps us towards is not the virtue itself but just this power of always trying again. For however important chastity (or courage, or truthfulness or any other virtue) may be, this process trains us in the habits of the soul which are more important still. It cures our illusions about ourselves and teaches us to depend on God.

Little did I know that God was not asking for a lifelong sexual fast (although I sometimes believed He was), but He wanted me to learn that I could not give in to my sexual instinct and satisfy my moral needs at the same time. He wanted me to exercise my freedom of choice as a moral being and all the while depend on Him. If I had known at the outset that I would attempt the virtue of chastity for five long years, I might have done something dramatic. As it was, I lived, as we all must live, one day at a time.

14

A Different Relationship

*. . . many leave their first marriages with the er-
roneous belief that a second union holds all they
have missed. But this is not reality. A second relationship . . . is dependent upon the maturity of the
people involved.*

When Don entered my life, I had been alone for four years.
During that time, God had helped me through the agony of
divorce, had shown me how to restructure my life, and had
taught me how to parent Lynn and Kathryn. Through His provision, I now had an ongoing career as an editor. In addition, I
felt good about myself as a mother and woman. In fact, never
in my thirty-two years had I felt better.

Don had also experienced some years alone. After his wife
told him she wanted a divorce, Don took a fairly typical route.
He went looking for affirmation from other women, and he left
his employer of twelve years. Although he had an excellent
position with a large Seattle firm, Don felt he needed additional career success. And so for three years he worked in a
different career field. A lawyer, he had no desire at that time to
go into private practice, but wanted instead to pursue success
in business.

Several months before we met, Don's position as the vice
president of a real estate firm soured. When we met, he was
selling commercial real estate, without notable success. For a
man who had sought success so relentlessly, these events,
coupled with a divorce, brought him to his knees. He realized,
moreover, that his relationships with women had not given
him what he desired. In a moment of truth, Don decided that

he could not continue in his present state any longer.

So for six weeks Don essentially retreated to his apartment, listened to music, read, and reflected. He only went out to work. Out of this experience, Don, who had been a nominal Christian most of his life, became a committed Christian. He emerged from his six-week retreat a changed man who was, at last, willing to trust God more completely.

Two months later, Don saw me in church, found out who I was, and called to ask me out. It was interesting that God brought us together in church. Both of us had looked other places for a meaningful relationship, only to discover the despair this experience can evoke. Both of us had concluded that we would no longer look for someone, but would trust God to bring the right person into our lives at the appropriate time.

This whole experience confirms what I now believe to be true about life. When we go in desperate pursuit of anything, be it husband, sex, or success, we give our own desires top priority in our lives. In so doing, we run the terrible risk of getting exactly what we want, only to find out later that it is not what is best for us. It is only as we trust God for everything that we will receive in life what we truly need; He alone knows what will make us happy.

Months before I met Don, I finally acknowledged to myself that I wished to remarry. About this time, a friend came to dinner. Jeanie was a widow and had been alone long enough to begin to contemplate remarriage. That night, after a warm, convivial evening, Jeanie suggested that if I did wish to remarry, I should make a list of specific characteristics that I desired in a second husband. While I scoffed at her suggestion (I thought this was a rather ridiculous thing to do), within minutes after Jeanie's car backed out of the driveway, I was propped up in bed with notebook and pencil in hand. In a short time, I constructed a three-page list that set forth some deep longings.

In the list I stated that I longed for an honest, faithful husband, who would sincerely put God above all else in his life.

Only in this way would there be any safety in our relationship. I knew from bitter experience how painful and dangerous it was to be married to a man whose world view was totally different from my own. So I asked for a man who had a strong ethical sense, which would allow him to make and keep a promise of fidelity. In addition I asked for the following characteristics:

1. That he be an affectionate, genuinely loving man. That he enjoy touching as well as intercourse, and that touching not be limited to the bedroom.

2. That he would be willing to become an involved, committed second father. That in the process he would be actively interested in the girls' educational, spiritual, and physical development. In addition, I hoped that he would grow to love the children in time.

3. That, as an intelligent, well-educated man, he would enjoy work and would be interested in career advancement, but his career would never be more important than the marriage or the family.

4. That he enjoy the books of C. S. Lewis. Since Lewis had influenced my thinking, I wanted to be able to share Lewis with a husband.

5. That, while athletic, he would not desert us for the ski slopes or for weekends of golf. I hoped to marry an active man who enjoyed the out-of-doors and who would teach the three of us to ski and sail.

6. Since I love to travel, I hoped to remarry someone who would feel that spending money for trips was acceptable. In addition, I hoped he would enjoy getting away frequently just as much as I do.

7. Moreover, I desired to marry a friendly man whose experience proved that he had the capacity to form intimate relationships. I did not want to marry an isolate who lacked communication skills.

Just to be honest, I added that I desired to marry a bachelor. I felt strongly that I did not want to remarry a divorced man who would bring an ex-wife and other children into our relationship. This was admittedly selfish, but I thought it wise. Why should we three have yet more people to deal with? Who needed the additional complications that ex-wives and children inevitably bring?

After I wrote the list, I placed it in a drawer and promptly forgot about it. I did, however, pray at intervals that God would send a second husband into my life. I wrote the list in September and began dating Don in March.

I later discovered that Don had also constructed his own list of characteristics that he desired in a wife. His list was considerably shorter than mine, but it included those characteristics he deemed important. For the first time in his life, he felt he wanted to marry a woman who was a real Christian. In addition, he stated that this person should be capable, possess a good self-image, enjoy the out-of-doors, relate well to his children, and have a life of her own. He wanted a wife who would be sexually attractive. Finally, he wanted to be able to accept this person just as she was, without any need to suggest change.

It was with some surprise and hilarity that we later compared our lists and discovered that God had given us most of what we asked for, and more. True, Don was not a bachelor, nor was I an earth mother.

And the presence of an ex-wife and children has created tension between us: It is no easy problem to negotiate. These four people do necessarily complicate our lives, as we must complicate theirs. So I was not granted my request in this one area. However, we concluded with gratitude that the vital areas were covered. Don felt, moreover, that my ability to be close was a characteristic he needed, but did not realize he should ask for. And I found in Don a characteristic that has rendered manifold benefits.

Don is the most stubborn man I have ever known. This quality, however, is coupled with tenderness and sensitivity to another person's feelings. Out of his stubborn humanity has come the most persistent human love I have ever experienced. He will love me, he does love me—no matter what. Instead of looking for ways to minimize his regard, Don uses his abundant energy and will to buttress the foundation of our relationship.

I must add at this juncture that our relationship got off to a slow start. When I met Don and found out that he had an ex-wife and children across town, I accepted him as a man whom I might date, but decided that I certainly did not want to become involved with him. Besides, he was a nice guy, and I was prejudiced against nice people. They were so concerned about seeking approval, I felt, that they did not know what they believed in, and consequently, they lacked depth. Since I had been accused of being an Amazon, I believed it would be disastrous to team up with a man who just might give in during any heated struggle. Just when I was ready to stop seeing Don, Katie and Barney came to visit me for three weeks.

In the presence of these good friends, I saw facets of Don's personality that had been cloaked in the dating situation. Also, I was able to check my perceptions against those of Katie and Barney. Did they think he could hold his own? Was he strong, firm under that nice and helpful exterior? Was he really committed to the values he espoused? Katie said that she believed he could become a strong man, if he were loved and affirmed, and that he was fast becoming a man of conviction.

Don had his own misgivings about me. Granted, I said I was a Christian, but what did that mean? Was I who I said I was, or was I simply putting my best foot forward to win a husband? Did I have a hidden agenda—an unacknowledged list of expectations? In other words, was my behavior a sham, and was I a liar?

Fortunately for our relationship, those three weeks with Katie and Barney provided a warm setting where we, each scarred by a marital failure, could begin to relax and get to know each other. Before Katie and Barney left for England, I knew that I loved Don, and Don thought that he loved me. He used the word *love* cautiously, and I respected him for that.

During the following seven-month period, Don and I worked through much suspicion, doubt, and fear—to hope and eventual trust. We discovered that we brought to the second relationship some leftover garbage from the first. Don did not believe that any woman could be genuinely honest, and I wondered about any husband's fidelity. So we tested each other. We talked hundreds of hours, we introduced each other to friends and checked their perceptions. Both of us were afraid of choosing badly and thereby experiencing a second marital failure.

In addition, we were psychologically bound to our first spouses. Don was all too ready to be helpful to his first wife, and on one occasion broke a date with me to accommodate her. I was angry and told him that he should either remarry her or become internally free. Thus, Don began to get his psychic divorce in earnest. Since I was still bound to Thomas by virtue of his rejection, Don's love began to heal that wound. As we grew closer to each other, we moved farther away from the remaining bonds of our first unions.

In the process, we found the best love affair of our lives. This new relationship gave us, in large measure, what we missed in our first marriages. I say this hesitantly, because I know that many leave their first marriages with the erroneous belief that a second union holds all they have missed. But this is not reality. A second relationship, just as a first, is dependent upon the maturity of the people involved. What Don and I have experienced are the attributes of a more mature relationship.

That we did not find this in our first marriages says more about who we were than about the quality of our first marital partners. We find that we accept each other as we are. This means that I accept Don's pleasant personality because I have found that he is not a weak man. He accepts my strength but feels I am more mouse than lioness.

Our relationship is founded upon unvarnished truth. We do

not lie to each other about the hard things of our lives or shirk the difficult subjects. Don knows about my difficulties with some people from his earlier life, and I have found him truthful.

We will pay any price to maintain closeness. Neither of us can stand cold silence. We have experienced continuing intimacy and we desire it. On occasion we have stayed up half the night to resolve an argument, and in the process I have come to respect Don's mettle.

One night, in my best theatrical style, I told him to leave. He refused. He added that he would leave, but only on his terms. Of course, I refused to accept his dictatorial terms, and so we sat in opposing chairs, staring at each other balefully. At about 3:00 A.M. my respect for Don tripled, and I became ready to negotiate. He was, after all, a reasonable man. When he left, our conflict had been resolved (we had both yielded some territory) and we were close.

How I have needed a man who does not run away in the face of conflict and negative feelings. For years, I longed for a person who would be there tomorrow. Although I knew that a neurotic fear of abandonment lay behind this, I felt that, after a period of testing, this area would be healed. It has been. And as a result I feel gratitude for this man whose persistent love has generated greater wholeness in me. And Don? Don, who described himself as a silent thirty-seven-year-old, wanted a close relationship with a woman. In addition, he desired a woman with good values, whom he could admire and respect.

One of God's good gifts to us during this time came in the person of Richard Langford. Doctor Langford, the senior minister at a Seattle church, became our counselor for a period of six months. When we felt that we would like to marry, we sought Dr. Langford out and asked if we could see him once a week and thereby work through some of the problems involved in remarriage.

I was primarily concerned about Don's children and what my relationship with them would be. I knew I would not be

Mother and did not like the role of the wicked stepmother. But was I friend, hostess, or what? When the children came to visit, we found it rough going. All the children were jealous and wary. I was no earth mother, and though I had good intentions, I found that Don's children conjured up some rather basic emotions. In addition, my children were quiet little girls, and Don's three were free spirits. Thus, we needed to discuss these issues and more in the presence of Dr. Langford.

Don wanted to make sure that we could resolve our problems and utilize good communication skills. At times Dr. Langford had the role of interpreting to Don what I tried to express, and vice versa. He helped us augment our rather basic skills and applauded our best efforts. When we had our regular disasters, he encouraged us and thus taught us much about God's love and forgiveness. We found this man ever in our corner. Doctor Langford is an encourager *par excellence*. Thus, with the help of this friend and minister, we moved steadily closer to marriage.

As our relationship deepened, Don's presence in my life enabled me to work through what had been for me a sordid and painful experience: Thomas's affair. And in the process, Don encouraged me to forgive Linda, for until that had occurred, we both knew I would never be free.

15
The Affair

To judge by literature, adultery would seem to be
one of the most remarkable of occupations in both
Europe and America.

DENIS DE ROUGEMONT

In our culture we have arrived at a point where affairs are
encouraged and in some real sense applauded. To engage in
an affair is to assert one's personhood, to make a statement, to
do one's own thing. Moreover, the media implies that affairs
do not generate significant pain or personal loss for any of the
participants.

Unfortunately, this is not true. Contrary to the media's approach, many do not find affairs glorious, passionate, and beautiful deeds. While the participants in an affair may experience
gains—sexual affirmation, for one—the wronged party has a
mountain of hurt to deal with. I wonder if an affair is ultimately anything but an injury.

When Thomas's affair became known, a new hell was introduced into my life. Whereas life before had contained hard
marital and personal struggles, life now was a struggle to survive. I hardly ate for two weeks. My anxiety was so great I
simply could not, at first, swallow food. Yet I had to continue
nursing my baby, and so for days I drank milk. In the process I
rapidly lost ten pounds.

I was overwhelmed with feelings of shame. *Who knows?* I
wondered. Since Thomas worked closely with Linda, I sur-
mised that some of his colleagues suspected that their relationship was more than casual. So when we went to any party
after that eventful weekend in September, I looked at the men

and women there and wondered how much they knew.

The greatest difficulty I had during those early months after the revelation of the affair was in continuing to live with a man I did not trust. Since Thomas still worked on the same floor with Linda at the medical center, I believed it was sheer folly to trust him. And what does one have when trust leaves a marriage? An anxious hell.

I have often wondered how marital partners regain trust once one of them has an affair, tells all the essential lies, and then because of guilt, comes clean. Does trust return once the commitment is renewed, or do the people live together for a long time without trust?

Someone suggested to me that, since trust is premised on communication, once communication is reestablished, trust will inevitably follow. With words and a turning to each other comes renewed trust. Another suggested that people who are going to continue to live together *must* trust each other. It simply takes too much energy to perpetuate a life of mistrust. I do not know the answer to this dilemma, but I do believe that only God can heal this wound. An affair creates a wounding that is so deep that only the Holy Spirit can possibly understand the pain, heal the persons involved, and restore trust to the marriage.

In addition to pondering how trust is restored, I have asked myself many times: Why did the affair occur? Obviously an affair does not just happen. Everyone appears to know that an affair is a symptom of an ailing marriage. Most agree that an affair does not occur in a union where two people feel that their needs are met and where they find personal fulfillment. Yet, ironically, during the early hours it is often difficult for the participants themselves to explain why an affair has taken place.

I have listened on several occasions as men have struggled to tell their wives why they had their affairs. No counselor, I was present shortly after these women discovered that their husbands had just had a first affair. I heard the men lamely attempt to remove some of the pain, to erase some of the seriousness of this act. I saw their wives physically resist their explanations. I concluded that the men did not know, at that moment, why they had had affairs. After the high tension passed, they would begin to uncover the reasons: the anger, the hurt, the resentment, the loneliness, the possible immaturity. But during the time when the affair became known, either the participants did not know why, or they refused to say.

In the early time, the wronged party is also bewildered. "Why did this happen?" and "How could he do this to me?" are the questions one asks during the early pain. The betrayed spouse feels rage, hurt, and no small amount of self-righteousness. One woman said that she also had ample opportunity to have affairs but had not done so. Thus, she was furious when her husband erred.

It is usually not until some time later that the betrayed husband or wife begins to seriously consider why. When this moment arrives, one must admit that he or she is somewhat responsible for the affair. It was hard for me to finally acknowledge that I had, with my anger and resentment, sent a needy husband out into a world full of sympathetic women. I was as responsible as Thomas for the sorry state of our marriage.

Thus, an affair is a shared responsibility. Both partners knowingly participated in an impoverished marriage and refused to correct marital ills. And as long as they live, either separately or together, the affair will be remembered, and that memory will produce pain. And so, an affair becomes a shared pain.

While bearing this pain in my person, I have tried over the years to understand how one arrives at the point where he decides to have an affair. Fortunately Thomas was honest with me on this score. One day while we still lived together, I came to him and said, "How did it happen?" Literature student that I was, I almost expected him to say that he had been caught in the grip of overwhelming passion. Thomas rather coldly dispelled this idea, and for that I was grateful. "It was quite simple," he said. "I decided to have an affair. It was an act of the will." His answer was consistent with what I have learned since then.

Thus, whenever I encounter someone, in literature or in life, who implies that passion rather than reason "made me do it," I inwardly resist. While this is a convenient rationalization, it is a rather hollow refrain. Affairs do not just happen; they are willed into existence. Prior to the affair there is a deliberate turning away from the spouse and a willful search for another person.

This turning away from the spouse as confidant, lover, source of comfort is a gradual thing. Obviously, some marriages are never close, and the parties never learn to communicate on more than a superficial level. But even in those marriages that are warm rooms, if one or both spouses choose to collect grievances, a wall is built. Then the marriage grows colder and lonelier. In this marital climate it becomes easy to imagine that in another union, or in an extramarital liaison, one will find a more understanding partner or better sex. This powerful fantasy, when linked with self-pity and the feeling that one deserves more from life, serves as impetus toward an affair.

And so the imagination capitulates before the will. Thomas à Kempis described this whole process hundreds of years ago in *The Imitation of Christ,* and his words still ring true:

> For first there cometh to the mind a bare thought of evil, then a strong imagination thereof, afterwards delight, and an evil notion, and then consent. And so by little and little our wicked enemy getteth complete entrance, because he is not resisted in the beginning. And the longer a man is slow to resist, so much the weaker doth he become daily in himself and the enemy stronger against him.

Thomas à Kempis is, of course, speaking about the nature of temptation, but he charts the course of capitulation well. Ovid said it yet another way: "Beginnings check, too late is physic sought."

What happens once an individual decides to have an affair? The obvious. The man or woman begins to search for the right partner. This search is not necessarily overt, nor is the person always aware that this is what he is about. But the messages transmitted between him and other women thereafter are different. And women other than his wife know that he is, as one lawyer put it, "prospecting." The search ends when the man finds the "right woman": i.e., one who is whatever the man feels he needs and cannot possibly find in his wife and who, because of her own needs, is open to such a relationship.

Thus is the affair launched. And I have talked to enough men and women who have had affairs to know that in the beginning many enjoy their extramarital liaisons. Said one man, "My affair was not dark and ugly; it was fun. Once again I experienced a romantic courtship after so many years in a hard marriage." He spoke of afternoons in the park, of poems, of gifts exchanged. Yet the fun has a less-publicized, darker side.

For a moment, let us look at the pain generated by an affair. If one has never experienced a spouse's affair, one cannot know how badly it hurts to be thus betrayed. We have no Richter scale for measuring human pain, and so we cannot evaluate at the outset how much injury the affair will cause. Those who have had affairs and have gone on to continued and perhaps improved marriages may applaud them. But I have yet to hear one person whose spouse had an affair state that the affair was a salutory experience and that all the pain was acceptable.

One man said that he had no idea that his wife would be so hurt by his affair that she would consider divorce. And I have a friend who told me that when she learned about her husband's first and only affair, she drove out to nearby mountains in the middle of the night to scream and howl. Only there, alone in the night, could she adequately vent her pain and rage. The pain of that rejection—for an affair is a rejection—is like no other. It conjures up enormous rage.

The Bible obviously understands the enormity of the hurt pride and the jealousy, for it speaks about adultery in Proverbs 6 and indicates that nothing can stand against a man's anger when his wife has been taken by another man. Further, the Bible indicates that ". . . whoso committeth adultery with a woman lacketh understanding: he that doeth it destroyeth his own soul. A wound and dishonour shall he get; and his reproach shall not be wiped away" (Proverbs 6:32, 33 KJV).

But leaving the pain behind and moving on, I believe affairs occur because of one main reason: We humans feel that we have a right to happiness. This right supersedes any promise of fidelity and any prior commitment. It took years for me to sort out this whole concept of one's inalienable right to happiness. Once again C. S. Lewis helped me. Lewis has a moving essay in *God in the Dock,* in which he explains why we give our sexual impulses such preposterous privilege. Says Lewis in this essay, "We Have No Right to Happiness":

> The sexual motive is taken to condone all sorts of behaviour which, if it had any other end in view, would be condemned as merciless, treacherous and unjust.

Then why do decent, law-abiding people engage in such potentially destructive behavior? Lewis argues that strong erotic passion promises everything:

> That possession of the beloved will confer, not merely frequent ecstasies, but settled, fruitful, deep-rooted, lifelong happiness. Hence all seems to be at stake. If we miss this chance we shall have lived in vain. At the very thought of such a doom we sink into fathomless depths of self-pity.

It is this all-or-nothing aspect of the affair that constitutes the lure. For who does not want strong love, settled bliss, the fulfillment of our talents and creative abilities? Our problem is that we look to another person to provide this for us. And since we are often unable to anticipate the ramifications of any particular course of action—we focus on the expected benefits and fail to count the cost—some seek in an affair all that is missing in their lives. Unfortunately, it is only after one has fallen over the precipice that one discovers the pain of falling into a deep pit.

The major question that two marital partners confront in the pit is whether or not they will continue their marriage. Each person must ask himself: Do I wish to slog through this morass of hurt and angry feelings in order to work on the problem areas of this marriage? Said one departing husband to his wife, "Why should I spend the next six years of my life sorting out this marriage, when I have found so much more with another woman?" Although this man left the other woman after a year, he raised a valid point. Few unhappy marriages can compete with what appears to be a beautiful affair.

Why is this so? At the time the affair occurs, the marriage may have had bad years and the participants much personal anguish. Communication has broken down, and resentment is high. Since beginnings can be beautiful, it is often hard for a person to give up a liaison which apparently has so much promise, to work on a scarred and battered marriage. To do so requires much commitment and maturity. The partner having the affair must take the longer view and forgo the immediate for the possibility of renewal in marriage. Few can do this. Some do not even desire to do this.

Obviously not all marriages end after the revelation of an affair. I have known couples whose marriages apparently absorbed the crisis the affair provoked. In each instance, the spouse having the affair did not wish to end the marriage, nor did the other partner retaliate by seeking an immediate divorce. And though each affair included sexual intercourse, it was clear that the people involved sought a loving, interested person, rather than just a sexual partner. Because of a strong marital commitment, each of these marriages not only survived, but with professional help, communication improved and intimacy deepened.

When marriages end after the revelation of an affair, however, they usually end on an exceedingly bitter note. A few months ago I read an unpublished article by a woman whose husband had left her for another woman. The writer ended her essay by saying that she would like to hurt her former husband as deeply as he has hurt her, but she does not believe it possible.

An affair hurts. It is a significant event in any human life and must be absorbed as part of a person's history. An affair shatters trust, either momentarily or forever, and it is the note on which many marriages end. Even if it renders what it promises—and I do not believe it possible—the cost in human pain is incalculable. Finally, an affair must be understood and ultimately forgiven. Only then can the people involved ever be healed.

16

The Other Woman

Will the lover with all his desires gratified continue to be in love with his Iseult once she had been wed?

DENIS DE ROUGEMONT

I have just talked to a woman on the phone whose husband had an affair some months ago. This wife is having to deal with all the agony associated with the knowledge that her husband, for whatever reason, has found someone else that he loves. Since I, too, have experienced that phenomenon called "the other woman," we discussed the process involved in coming to terms with this person. Said my friend, "I'm no longer comparing myself with her; I am putting her down."

"I know what that's like," I stated, "but you will have to go beyond that."

"I know," she said, and her voice grew quiet. And so she will, and in time perhaps the other woman will become a less potent factor in her continuing marriage. But that will take time, and the procedure is painful.

As I hung up the phone and came to the typewriter to rewrite this chapter, I thought of all the women I have met in these five years whose husbands sought other women. A significant number have been attractive and intelligent. Some were among the best and the brightest in their college classes. Yet all have suffered from the blow this act rendered to their self-esteem. All have spent much time in coming to terms with their husbands' affairs.

Possibly no marital act affects the self-esteem as deeply as having a spouse choose someone else to love. I do not care whether the involvement is emotional or sexual or both. The fact remains: I, the wife, am in some area of my life found wanting. And at first, nothing the husband can say to soothe the wound helps, for the wife knows in her soul that if she had been enough or had been perceived as enough, he would not have strayed.

When I discovered that my husband had become involved with someone else, I entered the first stage in the process termed *dealing with the other woman.* I was overwhelmed with feelings of inadequacy. No matter that for thirty years I had considered myself an attractive woman with a better-than-average intelligence. My husband had chosen her, so she had to be something I was not. I began to compare myself with her.

Although she was pretty, I honestly did not think she was better looking than I was. I concluded, moreover, that I was better educated. But she had to be better. In what way? I quizzed my husband, and he was, thank God, silent. I wracked my brain. Was she more supportive? Ah, that was it. She had listened to my husband and had given him emotional support during a difficult year of residency. And well she might, my anger countered. She was not married to him and consequently did not have the frustrations that were mine. But that line of reasoning did not help.

For a while nothing helped. The reason is that a husband's affair touches a woman where she lives—inside her head and body. What I valued, what I believed, were obviously insignificant. I had not been able to challenge and hold my husband. What I was, was simply not enough. Never mind that he was no Mr. Atlas. Since he had rejected me for someone else, for a time I had to deal with that.

I remember, with genuine compassion, the woman I was during that early time after the revelation of the affair. For months I could hardly bear to look in the mirror, except to scrutinize my face and body and ask, *Why?* Because of my wounded self-esteem, I changed the kind of clothes I wore. I,

who love the elegant and conservative styles featured in
Vogue, became more provocative in my dress. It was some
time before I reaffirmed the subtle colors and classic styles
that I love.

This was also the time I bleached my hair. One weekend I
purchased one of those do-it-yourself frosting kits and did
such a drastic job on my hair that I, a natural brown, soon
looked like a newborn chicken. My whole head ached as I saw
that dry, yellow down in the mirror. The next day I paid a
small fortune for a reverse frosting at the hairdresser's. This
one act symbolized how bruised I was inside and how willing
I was to deny my own sense of self in order to woo Thomas
back or, at minimum, bolster a flagging ego.

The comparisons did not cease until much later, when a
friend wisely said, "You are doing yourself a great disservice,
Brenda. The other woman was not chosen because she was
better; she was chosen because she was there. If it had not
been her, it would have been someone else." Only as that
thought began to penetrate did I move on to the next stage in
the process. I began to see her as less than myself.

In my mind I attacked her honesty or lack of it, her willingness to compromise her integrity. How could she have gotten
involved with a married man and end her own marriage in the
process? Had she no loyalty to her husband of so many years,
the father of her children? In short, I was obsessed by her and,
in truth, I hated her.

Long after I had forgiven Thomas, I was still unwilling to
forgive Linda. Perhaps I could not forgive her because I er-
roneously blamed her for the divorce, believing in my heart
that Thomas might not have gone if he had not had someone
conveniently waiting for him. Or perhaps I felt that to forgive
the whole wrong was to condone the wrong.

It became exquisitely painful, however, to maintain my
hatred when my children began to visit their father after his
remarriage. They grew to like this woman called Linda, while
I could hardly bear to hear them mention her name, as they

certainly did when they returned from their long summer visits. They spoke of all the comfort she had given, of activities she had supervised, of kindness bestowed. As I listened to their tales, the ice around my heart began to melt.

Moreover, God kept pressing me to forgive this woman. My future husband also urged me to rid myself of this hatred. And so, as the time of my remarriage approached, I sensed that the moment had finally come to discard this heavy baggage.

Impulsively, I dialed Linda's number on the telephone. By this time I had not spoken to her for nearly five years. I had called her only once before, on the day the affair was revealed, to ask her if she intended to marry Thomas. And now, five years later, I was again dialing the other woman. Within seconds she answered the phone. Her voice was clear and strong. After I identified myself, I started my recital.

"Linda," I said, "you have probably heard that I am getting married again."

"Yes," she said expectantly.

"Well, I want to tell you that the slate is clean between us. I am no longer bitter toward you for your involvement in the end of my marriage."

She was gracious and kind. She listened to my recital, and we chatted briefly. She told me that she almost felt she knew me, because the girls had spoken of me so often. I told her that they talked about her as well, liked her, and that I appreciated all that she had done for them. I added that what had happened had hurt me deeply: I had loved Thomas for a long time after the marriage ended. Nothing, I added, but Christ could provide the bridge between us. Humanly speaking, I could never overlook what happened and pretend that it did not affect me deeply.

She appeared to understand and thanked me for calling. When I hung up the phone, I was full of joy. Energy flooded my whole body. I sat down and wrote twelve letters to friends, telling them about the freedom that had been five years in coming. That one phone call brought incredible psychological freedom. It was as if creativity and joy had been dammed up for years and forgiveness provided instantaneous release. No longer was I obsessed with this person called Linda: In fact, the other woman lost her larger-than-life dimension and became at that moment just another person, not that unlike myself.

The thought came fleetingly that had we met under different circumstances, I might have liked Linda and wanted her to be my friend. She seemed sensitive, intelligent, perceptive. I was struck by the irony of our situation. Here we are, two people who might have been drawn to each other under different circumstances, but who will never be able to relate to each other in any meaningful way. Yet, because of the children, we will remain on the periphery of each other's lives for the rest of our days.

After I had forgiven Linda, I was then ready for the third step in the healing process. I was ready to see her in a more realistic perspective and become more objective about the phenomenon called the other woman. Although our culture and some literature tend to give the other woman a place of strength and preeminence, I think this is erroneous. The other woman, contrary to popular belief, is not superhuman, super-sexual, super-*anything*. She is simply another human being, with her own particular history and need, and it is her need, and not her strength, that propels her into the relationship.

I did not always believe thus. When Thomas had the affair, I labored under the illusion that he and Linda had at last experienced the great romance. A student of literature and an incurable romantic, I cast their affair more in terms of the Tristan and Iseult myth of the twelfth century than the banal Hollywood films about adultery.

As I tuned in to the media, what I heard and read pandered to my fantasy. The spouse who has an affair is often portrayed as a person of great capacity, who is misunderstood or unappreciated. The other woman is that illusive, all-nurturing, all-encompassing eternal woman. At her breast the beleaguered husband experiences transports of mystical passion. Only the

wife suffers from a negative portrayal. She is viewed as with-
holding, inadequate, and guilty. If it were not for her, no man
would wander.

And so the man leaves in pursuit of the other woman, his
Iseult. But does Iseult exist? Is there a woman alive who can
perpetually fan the fires of passion and provide any man all
that his heart desires? I do believe that men believe Iseults
exist outside of their marriages, just as some women are con-
stantly on the lookout for a Tristan. Both Iseult and Tristan are
the unattainable, or at least the forbidden, if one is safely inside a marriage. But let us suppose, for the sake of argument,
that Iseults and Tristans exist in abundance. What if a man
gets his divorce and marries his Iseult. What then? Denis de
Rougemont writes in *Love in the Western World:*

> Will the lover with all his desires gratified continue to
> be in love with his Iseult once she had been wed? Is a
> cherished nostalgia still desirable once it has recovered
> its object? For Iseult is ever a stranger, the very essence
> of what is strange in woman and of all that is eternally
> fugitive, vanishing and almost hostile in a fellow being,
> that which indeed incites to pursuit, and rouses in the
> heart of a man who has fallen a prey to the myth an
> avidity for possession so much more delightful than
> possession itself.

Denis de Rougemont suggests that should a man marry his
Iseult, he will either create fresh obstructions in their union so
that he can renew the struggle for passion, or he will have
successive love affairs. Yet "How patent the degradation of a
Tristan who has *several* Iseults!"

Since this chapter is about the other woman, the Iseult, I
would like to imagine what happens to her after she woos the
husband away from his wife. Does she live ever after in marital bliss? What guarantee does she have that this union will be
happy and fulfilling?

What I have to say now I need to say with some compassion,

realizing that during early separation, I came close to being the other woman. I do not believe the other woman will ever again have an easy life. From the moment she decides to become involved in someone else's marriage, she settles for less than the best that life can offer her. She dons the role of the other woman, the usurper, and this must somehow be absorbed into her picture of herself.

Even if the love she shares with this formerly married man is the best she has ever known, is it all that it might have been, had she met this person, or someone else, under different circumstances?

The other woman has her own unique dilemma. She has no assurance that further down the pike her husband will not be wooed and won by someone else. While some women are concerned about their husband's fidelity, the other woman has proof of her husband's capacity for infidelity. She banks on the hope that, for whatever reason, her husband will be faithful to her. This hope must be a fragile thing, at best.

And what about the marriage the other woman enjoys? When the romance exists in life instead of literature, what then? Probably the lovers eventually end up in suburbia, paying off mortgages, raising children, and cooking eggs—like the rest of us. Since all relationships mature and change, the romance—if legalized—is eventually tried and tested in the marital fire. And it is ultimately as difficult for great lovers to maintain a high pitch of erotic passion as it is for those who never had affairs, but chose instead the more pedestrian way of fidelity within one marriage.

C. S. Lewis says it well in *God in the Dock:* "When two people achieve lasting happiness, this is not solely because they are great lovers but because they are also—I must put it crudely—good people; controlled, loyal, fairminded, mutually adaptable people."

Also, since the other woman is possessor of a conscience, she cannot commit a wrong and go her way scot-free. Last night I finished reading a book written by a woman who was the other woman in numerous, uncommitted relationships. The writer spoke of her aimlessness, her guilt, and deep sense of inner ruin. I felt a strong sense of sympathy for this person, since I have also known loneliness. And as I read, I saw that we all must find our way to God if we are ever to fully love and respect ourselves. Thus, while the rejected wife certainly has her months and years of personal pain, the other woman must have her years of guilt.

Thus my view of the other woman has changed dramatically since those early days of pain. She is no longer a threat, nor is she someone to be hated. I see that the other woman is made of the same raw human material that I am. Since we are all vulnerable and are all human size, it is well that we view one another with forgiveness and some compassion. For who knows in the end who has the harder life—the other woman or the rejected wife?

I wish to share an idea that has brought much healing to my bones. It is simply this: No human being can ever be replaced in another's life. Displaced, yes; replaced, no. Henry the Eighth of England had six wives, but they were six totally different women, and Catherine of Aragon was always his first wife. The other woman, while she may be *best* wife, will never be *first* wife. She is second, third, or fourth wife, or she may never become wife at all. Although part of the rejected wife's concern is that the other woman will replace her by being all that she was and more, this does not happen. The other woman is simply another, unique person, with her own particular foibles, needs, and gifts. She and her lover know that she has not replaced the former wife after all: She has merely come after her in line.

That awareness has profoundly comforted me. When I realized that I could never be eradicated from Thomas's personal history, that I would always be his first wife and the mother of his first children, I let him go. Moreover, the hurt began to fade. We cannot, thank God, eradicate any segment of our lives or any person we have ever loved, no matter how hard we try. We can accept their role in our past and move on.

17

Remarriage

Remarriage is always related to the renewing
grace of God, which meets a person in his or her
failure and grants another chance.

DWIGHT HERVEY SMALL

When Don and I were married the first time, each of us had
a traditional wedding. Don, a mature twenty-six, was married
a few days after he finished law school. Then he and his bride
honeymooned across America enroute to a new job and home.
Thomas and I were married in a stately church in the South
three days after we graduated from college. At each wedding
the bride wore white, the relatives congregated, and all the
usual rituals were observed.

When Don and I approached our second wedding, we were
relieved that minimal rituals existed to be observed. To date,
the etiquette experts have refrained from charting the course
for second marriages. Thus, older, freer, we planned a wedding that would reflect our personalities rather than society's
expectations. As we talked, we realized that we wanted to be
married in a home rather than a church. We knew that friends
rather than relatives would most likely attend (because of cost
and distance), and we wanted a warm experience rather than a
coldly formal wedding.

With this in mind, we asked my Seattle "family," John and
Penny, if we could be married in their home. They were
pleased, and Penny immediately started to scrub her house to
get it into immaculate condition for our wedding. And we
asked the man who knew us best to conduct the service. We
told Dr. Langford that we wanted him to preach a sermon that

would deal honestly with the fact that we were divorced and yet speak of God's forgiveness and power to heal.

In addition, we wanted to be married at the start of a new day. When I was in Switzerland years before, I heard of a wedding that occurred beside an Alpine stream early in the morning, and I later hiked to the place. I responded to the symbolism of a new beginning in a marriage which would occur at the beginning of the day. So we asked our fifty friends to sacrifice their Saturday morning and come to a wedding at the early hour of nine o'clock. We promised to feed them after the ceremony, but asked each family to bring a coffee cake, since we would provide the rest. Don and Penny's husband, John, thought they would enjoy cooking bacon and eggs; Penny and I agreed to serve.

We decided that all five children should attend the ceremony, since any second union affected them. We knew from our many conversations with all five youngsters that this wedding was a hard and somewhat frightening event for them. Since all had grown accustomed to relating to us as single parents, they found it difficult to deal with a strange adult and other children.

Increasingly, Don and I had to deal with the jealousy that the children felt toward one another and the usurping stranger. Don's children feared they were losing a father; they had no firm idea (although we tried to reassure them) about what their place would be in the new family. Although Lynn and Kathryn liked Don, they were not at all sure they wanted him to come and live with us. They simply did not want to share their mommy with any man. But as the day approached, the apprehension was momentarily pushed aside, and the children seemed genuinely excited about the pending event.

The night before the wedding was a curious experience. Although I felt excitement at the prospect of this new life, I was anxious and saddened, as well. During the day, friends had called from England, and some had sent telegrams. Those who knew us rejoiced with us that God had given us this opportunity to create and enjoy a new marriage. But during the aloneness of that evening, I realized that an era of my life was ending.

As I tucked Lynn and Kathryn into bed, admired their new dresses, and answered their questions, they began to cry softly. "I don't want you to get married again," wailed five-year-old Lynn. "I don't want our family to change and grow larger," said Kathryn, struggling to control herself. Just as I had done on countless occasions in the past, I took the children into my arms and tried to comfort them, but soon I was crying, too.

We three recognized that while the future would bring new happiness into our lives, nonetheless the marriage would usher in many changes. And changes are hard to negotiate, especially when life has been full of them. For five years I had been the single most important parent to my children. Although they loved their biological father, they lived with me. I was the person who had always been there. Now they would have to share me with someone else. And though Don had been in their young lives for nearly a year, they did not know him well. In addition, they dreaded the week of the honeymoon, when they would be away from me.

As I comforted my children, I realized that I had my own dilemma to deal with. For five years I had been alone, and my major source of love, comfort, and help had been God. He had entered my life with greater force and clarity at a time when Thomas left us to cope with life alone. Our needs had always been met during those five years and, in addition, God had given me many of the desires of my heart. I had traveled extensively, had lived in England, had met many loving people. I wondered: Will this relationship change as I necessarily transfer some dependence from God to Don? And yet I recognized that Don himself had come as an answer to prayer and the deeper longing in my heart to love and be loved by a man.

And so I told the girls goodnight, picked up my worn Bible,

and took my questions to bed. I awoke early on the day of my second wedding and, turning on the light, I flipped through the Bible until I found a passage that caught my attention. I noted with no small amount of humor that the passage was about an imminent death, rather than a wedding. The words were Joshua's and he was reminding the Israelites of what God had been to them in the past and of all He would continue to be in the future. Said Joshua:

> Today I am going the way of all the earth; and you know with all your hearts and souls that not one of all the good promises which the Lord your God made to you has failed. They all came to pass for you . . . .
>
> Joshua 23:14

I realized that just as God had not failed me in the past, He would not fail me today, or ever. He provided the continuity between those five years alone and any future. Comforted, I prepared to welcome the day.

On that day I experienced my happiest wedding. At nine o'clock Don and I were waiting inside the door of John and Penny's home to greet our friends, who rushed into the warm house. Seattle was clear and cold that February morning. The children were animated and pleased with their new clothes and flowers. They rushed around, meeting all who came.

In planning our wedding, Don and I decided to give two short talks at the conclusion of Dr. Langford's sermon: One address to each other, another to our assembled friends. Don planned this part of the service carefully, because he wanted all to know just what our marriage, and the occasion, meant to him. I complied with his idea, but was not in the least excited about the prospect of giving a speech at my own wedding. I felt I would be nervous and wooden in anything I said. But we told Dr. Langford about Don's desire, and he endorsed the plan.

On that February morning Dr. Langford gave a moving sermon about the possibility of second chances. Loving as always, he stated that Don and I had both experienced the pain that comes from division and sin in our first marriages, and though God always holds up the standard of perfection for the Christian life, nonetheless the Bible tells of many second chances. He then noted the presence of the five children and stated that any new marriage included them and necessitated a loving commitment to them. When he turned and talked to our children, all sat a little straighter and listened intently.

After the sermon and the vows, Don turned to me for the first half of his talk. He told all assembled that, in any list of priorities, he would place our relationship second after God, but before any worldly success. In addition, he promised that when trouble came, he would not run away. A few of my friends, knowing my needs, cheered quietly at this point. At the end of his loving and moving talk, Don gave me the floor.

Turning to Don, I promised that I would live with him in love and honesty. I added that I would work at communication and, whenever necessary, ask his forgiveness.

Then I turned to our friends and told them that Don and I had awakened at 4:00 A.M. that day—in separate houses—and that I had experienced some anxiety about whether or not we were doing the right thing. I said that I had asked many people, including the milkman, for reassurance, but had ultimately found it in God. I read the verse that friends from L'Abri had wired: "No good thing does the Lord withhold from those who walk uprightly" (*see* Psalms 84:11 KJV), and added that a chapter of my life was ending.

I stated that Don and I were under no illusions about our ability to create and sustain a viable union. We had both known the pain and brokenness of divorce. Yet we believed that at the point of our inadequacy, God's adequacy would begin.

When I finished, Dr. Langford, who had either forgotten that Don was due to speak again, or who had become flustered by the audience's response, said, "Let us pray." I looked at Don with surprise, and before we knew it, the service was over. Dear Don was left with the feeling that I had upstaged him. From that day he determined that if we ever spoke together in the future (and we would, many times), he would go first and make sure that he had said all he wished to say before he turned the podium over to me. Wise man.

The only sadness I felt on this wedding day had to do with our children. As our friends departed and Don's three were taken home, there was a sense of quiet and lostness about them. They looked so vulnerable as they huddled in the back of Ed's car. Lynn and Kathryn were openly depressed as they prepared to go to Olympia for the week. They tried to be brave in front of the adults, but they let me know privately that this occasion was hard for them. They felt that this whole experience was just too painful, and so once again I drew them close, promised to call them several times, and added that I would pray for them daily. They knew the Riggans well, had always loved spending weekends with them before, but for the first time they were going to Olympia without me.

As I watched them trundle off and climb into the Riggans' car, I realized anew just how much is required of all our children, who have so little to say about their parents' divorces and remarriages. At a time when they are young and vulnerable and so dependent on parents to make the universe a safe place, their uncertain parents move in and out of relationships meant to be permanent with alarming speed. They often conclude there is no safe place, and these grown-ups just may not know what they are doing.

If I did not trust a God who heals and is the all-nurturing parent, I would long ago have despaired for my little children. But I have watched Him bind up wounds that life and we, their parents, inflicted. Now, as earlier, I placed my beautiful, sad children in His hands. Trusting Him and the good care of our friends, I turned to my husband.

We walked back to John and Penny's house for a quiet cup of coffee with these friends before we left for our honeymoon. We were reluctant to move on, and for a time sat and savored the moment. The fun and the joy of the morning lingered as we talked in front of the fire. It was noon when Don and I finally left their house to begin our marriage.

As we drove away that early afternoon, both of us felt excitement about our new life and gratitude for all that God had done. We, who had known marital failure and the death of dreams, believed that we had been given a new beginning, a new opportunity to experience a different quality of marriage, a different kind of life. We looked to the future with anticipation and joy.

Epilogue

Experience is not what happens to you; it is what
you do with what happens to you.

ALDOUS HUXLEY

Once again the year has come full circle, and it is early
September. One year ago, sitting on the patio in full sunlight, I
started to write this book, and in so doing embarked on a
journey. That journey has caused me to relive those early
hours and years of separation and divorce and has brought me
to the present moment of marital joy. And since it is September, today marks another aniversary: Seven years ago the
telephone rang, and an unknown male voice ushered in an
experience that, for a time, shattered my life.

How strange life is. We, who think we are gods and god-
desses, have so little ultimate control over the circumstances
of our lives. We seldom end up in our thirties and forties at
that place we envisioned for ourselves in our youth. Rather we
wander down unknown roads we would not have dreamed of
taking at the beginning of our journey. And we experience so
much that we would never have chosen as either good or
necessary for the fleshing out of our humanity.

During my early twenties I never thought that I would be
divorced and adrift at thirty. Raise my children alone? Never.
I, who had known such a lonely childhood, wanted only nor-
malcy, whatever that was, above all else. I thought that the
good life included a reasonably successful marriage, a pro-
ductive career, and the rearing of good and honest children.
With these limited aspirations, I planned to live a tidy life
(with absolutely no breath of scandal) and enjoy the fruits of
my labors.

I did not know how I would do this. Nor was I aware of the

psychological deficits and problems I brought to my marriage. Nor did I know my first husband in any meaningful sense. Granted, I knew about him, and I knew what he told me. But how naive we both were. And how little I wanted out of life. I would have gone haltingly into middle age, deprived of growth and self-awareness, if, in the process, I could have avoided any significant suffering.

But that was not to be. Instead I suddenly became a woman alone. Pitting every resource, inner and outer, against the world, I found that with God's help I could not only raise good and honest children, but I could help them become happy. During those five years alone, I shed much anxiety about myself and my ability to cope with the world. Moreover, I found to my delight that I could form good friendships, make ethical decisions, create a viable life-style, and enjoy a career. Thus, I, who would have fled the suffering inherent in separation and divorce, have learned that precisely because I have suffered, I have grown.

This is not to say, as the culture contends, that if divorce produces growth it is therefore good. I do not believe this at all. If anything, my bias is against divorce and for marital health and continuity. But divorce, as any other life crisis, presents one with the option: Grow or be destroyed. There is, apparently, no middle ground, for the problems and the emotions that divorce generates are intense. I chose to grow.

And in the process of confronting self and life, I have come to realize that I could also have grown within the confines of my first marriage. Since this alternative was foreclosed, I have chosen to make good out of the apparent evil of divorce. This has not occurred without effort on my part or without God's help. At any point, save for the grace of God, I might have opted for bitterness and the half-life of regret. It suits my melancholy nature far better than the stoical attitude of going on.

But I did go on and subsequently learned many valuable lessons. For one, I will never again fear life alone without a man. Some women, who have never had to face their existential aloneness, move into middle age terrified of the moment when they might lose their husband to death, or worse, to divorce. Their vulnerability is painfully real. Unprepared to cope with life alone or the possibility of earning a living, they are crippled by their fears.

Yet the one great lesson of life is that we need not be destroyed by anything life renders. The Christian knows, or will learn, that in any aloneness, in any need, he has but to turn around and find that God is there.

Thus, the years that brought the death of my first marriage have brought ultimate good. Not only have I shed fears, as the butterfly sheds the constricting cocoon, but I have experienced the first joy of my life. Joy appeared to me first in the form of Christian community and for the last year and a half has come as part of this second marriage. When we finally experience joy (and I believe that only with God is this possible) we learn to let the ephemeral and fickle happiness go and wait for something better.

Joy has not always come easily. Both Don and I are stubborn, strong personalities who like to run the show. Since the problems that attend second marriages are complex, we have had many rough areas to negotiate. But we work hard to maintain good feelings. Knowing that, as humans, we have only so much time and energy, Don and I established priorities early on. And as a result, we judiciously guard our time together. Since we have two children who live with us, we hold sacrosanct those hours of each day when we four come together to live as a family. It is this caring for the inner life of our marriage that has rendered so much joy. And as the marriage is nurtured, it becomes stronger.

Further, I know that God is daily at work in our union. It is not, thank God, entirely up to us. Marriage is no union of saints. It is the yoking of two fallible people. Believing that God brought us together, that He has given us this second opportunity to experience marriage as He intended it, we realize that we are in school, and class is always in session. Some aspects of the learning process are good fun; others are extremely hard.

I have had to learn to bend and yield in this marriage, as I refused to do in the first. Don has had to learn to put in the hours to forge a close relationship, hours that he formerly gave to a career. God appears to have a goal in all of this: It is as if He takes us over the rough terrain of past failure and tells us, "With My help you will not fail again."

And so we grow as we daily confront ourselves. And when we meet in our bed each night for what one friend calls the best part of the day, then the overwhelming feeling that we have is one of gratitude for this second chance.

James Barrie, in his story of Peter Pan entitled "Lock Out Time," speaks negatively about the possibility of second chances. Peter, who had fled his home to go to Kensington Gardens, returns to his mother's window, only to discover that she has a new little boy and that the window is barred against his reentry. Barrie writes:

> He had to fly back, sobbing to the Gardens, and he never saw his dear again. What a glorious boy he meant to be to her. Ah, Peter, we who have made the great mistake, how differently we should all act at the second chance . . . . there is no second chance, not for most of us. When we reach the window it is Lock Out Time. The iron bars are up for life.

Not so, dear Barrie, not so. I read and believed those words years ago, in the first hours alone. Now I know and have experienced the joy of the second chance. The iron bars are not up for life. We suffer, we forgive, we grow, and we do love again. This time, because of our gratitude, the love is better, truer. When we lose what we hold dear, what we prize most highly, we then learn to value all the gifts of life. And I think somehow God would have it so.

Helen Timmons
621 Monroe St
Fremont O